ALL THE BEST MUFFINS
AND QUICK BREADS

Cookbooks by Joie Warner
ALL THE BEST PASTA SAUCES
ALL THE BEST SALADS
ALL THE BEST PIZZAS
ALL THE BEST CHICKEN DINNERS
ALL THE BEST MEXICAN MEALS
ALL THE BEST MUFFINS AND QUICK BREADS
ALL THE BEST POTATOES
ALL THE BEST COOKIES
ALL THE BEST PASTA SAUCES II
ALL THE BEST RICE
THE COMPLETE BOOK OF CHICKEN WINGS
THE BRAUN HAND BLENDER COOKBOOK
A TASTE OF CHINATOWN
JOIE WARNER'S SPAGHETTI
JOIE WARNER'S CAESAR SALADS
JOIE WARNER'S APPLE DESERTS

ALL THE BEST

MUFFINS
and QUICK BREADS

BY

JOIE WARNER

HEARST BOOKS • New York

A FLAVOR BOOK

Recognizing the importance of preserving what has
been written, it is the policy of William Morrow and
Company, Inc., and its imprints and affiliates to have
the books it publishes printed on acid-free paper, and
we exert our best efforts to that end.

LIBRARY OF CONGRESS CATALOGING-IN-PUBLICATION DATA
Warner, Joie.
    All the best muffins and quick breads/by Joie Warner.
        p.   cm.
Includes index.
ISBN 0-688-11658-2
1. Muffins.   2. Bread.   I. Title.   II. Title: Muffins and
quick breads.
TX770.M83W37   1992
641.8'15-dc20   92-14209
                                                CIP

Printed in the United States of America

    3 4 5 6 7 8 9 10

This book was created and produced by

Flavor Publications, Inc.
208 East 51st Street, Suite 240
New York, New York 10022

CONTENTS

INTRODUCTION

MUFFINS ARE MARVELOUS. They're delicious, nutritious, incredibly versatile, inexpensive, and simple to prepare – the perfect food for busy cooks.

Though Americans have doted for decades on muffins, today, it seems, everyone is truly mad about muffins. Muffin shops abound, sporting an incredible variety of flavors from fragrant lemon to savory chick-pea. Bed-and-breakfast inns across the nation are famous expressly for the mouthwatering muffins they serve their guests at breakfast-time.

It's easy to understand the growing popularity of these small, delightful cakes: fresh and warm, just-baked muffins are simply a wonderful way to start the day; to serve with tea or snacks, or to enjoy at lunch or dinner. Quick breads, too, are gaining in favor. Why wait for a yeast bread to rise when delicious breads are as easy to make as their muffin cousins? Quick breads, too, have an endless range of flavors and textures, from sweet to savory, featuring natural ingredients from grains, nuts, seeds, and herbs, to fresh and dried fruits and vegetables.

Both muffins and quick breads are the easiest of baked goods to prepare, so there is absolutely no need to serve the store-made variety. Instead of yeast, they rely on baking powder and/or baking soda for a light and tender dough. With no rising time necessary, muffins and quick breads are a superlative fast food. And, with the basic staples almost always on hand – flour, baking powder, sugar, eggs, and milk, as well as one special ingredient such as dried apricots or what have you, it is just a simple matter of mixing the dry ingredients in one bowl, the liquid ingredients in another, then gently folding them to combine. The batter is mixed and usually ready to bake in less than 10 minutes: just the time needed to heat your oven. The batter is then spooned into lightly-greased pans and baked for about 20 minutes for muffins, an hour for quick breads. (And, since the arrival of nonstick pans and cooking spray, muffin and bread making is even more incredibly fast and convenient.)

An added bonus: the ingredients can be mixed in their separate bowls several hours or up to a day before baking (refrigerating the liquid ingredients, of course, and not adding the melted butter until the last minute), and then combined at the last minute to emerge, right on time, fresh and warm from the oven.

No special techniques or equipment are needed to bake muffins or quick breads. They are infinitely adaptable and offer endless possibilities for the cook. You can use any flour and grain – white, rye, whole wheat, buckwheat, soy flour, rice flour, oats, cornmeal, wheat bran, oat bran, and seeds – to name a few. Naturally, when made with whole-grain flour, they are at their healthiest and most vitamin-packed. And with the addition of eggs and milk, most muffins and quick breads have more nutritional punch than most yeast breads. As well, the addition of dried or fresh fruit, vegetables, nuts, and bran will give you a high-fiber muffin or bread.

To sweeten muffins or quick breads, anything from white and brown sugar to honey, maple syrup, molasses – even frozen fruit juice concentrates – can be used. Sweeteners are necessary to tenderize, flavor, and help the bread cook properly. Often, less sweetener is used when savory muffins or breads are prepared, making them even more nutritious and good for you.

You cannot prepare muffins or breads without some kind of oil or fat such as butter, vegetable oil, or vegetable shortening. It is required for tenderness, volume, texture, and fullness of flavor. And finally, the liquid ingredients – eggs, water, milk, or fruit juice – provide the wet – or binding – ingredients.

Muffins and quick breads are definitely a boon for the cook who wants to serve delicious, homey breads at a moment's notice.

They also make the loveliest of gifts to present to friends, particularly when prettily wrapped and tied with a ribbon.

I hope you enjoy my collection of muffin and quick bread recipes – from sweet treats to healthy delights prepared with fresh, natural ingredients. You'll discover – if you haven't already – that homemade muffins and quick breads are always appreciated, no matter what the occasion.

JOIE WARNER

♦ ♦ ♦

BASICS

READ THE RECIPE AND GATHER INGREDIENTS

The secret to successful cooking and baking is to read the recipe before you begin in order to familiarize yourself with the equipment, techniques, and ingredients required to complete the recipe without interruption. Gather your equipment – bowls, spatula, spoons, measuring cups, baking pans – and ingredients to make sure you have everything at hand. As you are gathering the ingredients, prepare them as you go – chopping, grating, or slicing – as required. Nothing is more frustrating than getting part way through the recipe only to find that you don't have a crucial ingredient, haven't completed an important procedure, or don't have the proper size pan.

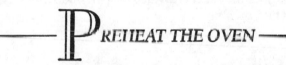

PREHEAT THE OVEN

Muffins and quick breads must be placed in a thoroughly preheated oven for maximum rise. Each of the following recipes gives the particular heat required for each recipe. Too little heat will produce flat muffins or breads – too high a heat will produce overbrowned breads with uncooked centers. Always adjust the oven rack to the top third position for maximum heat.

PANS

Muffin pans come in varying capacities. Regular pans hold anywhere from ¼ cup to ½ cup batter, miniature muffin pans hold about 2 tablespoons. Any of the following recipes can be baked as minimuffins; just remember to reduce baking times if doing so. Quick bread recipes using 2 cups of flour will fit a standard 8- or 9-inch rectangular loaf pan or two 5-inch small loaf pans.

GREASING THE PAN

If you plan to bake a lot of muffins and quick breads, I highly recommend nonstick muffin and loaf pans. These pans need only a light greasing with vegetable spray, making muffins or breads a breeze to remove and the pans easy to clean. To grease pans (nonstick pans still do require a light greasing), vegetable spray is the quickest and most convenient, or use melted butter or vegetable oil. (Or you may prefer to use paper or foil baking cups.) If using regular pans, they should be greased very well so that the inside surface is thoroughly coated – don't forget the top surface for muffins that rise above the pan. If the recipe makes less than the muffin pan, prepare only the number needed and once the batter is divided properly, add a little water to those not being used to prevent scorching.

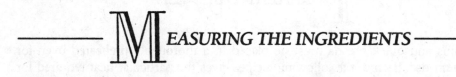

MEASURING THE INGREDIENTS

Dry ingredients should always be measured in nested measuring cups. Scoop up the ingredient – such as flour or sugar – and, using the straight edge of a knife, level the dry ingredients by scraping off the excess. Dry and powdered ingredients such as baking powder and salt are measured with measuring spoons. Fill the spoons to overflowing, then level as described above. Liquid ingredients should be measured with spouted liquid measuring cups that are marked off in quarters and thirds. Add the liquid to the exact markings, then check by putting the cup on a level surface and viewing straight on.

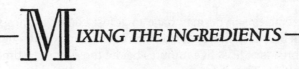

MIXING THE INGREDIENTS

Muffins are prepared in one of two ways – folded or creamed. Folded muffins are the most common. The liquid mixture and dry ingredients are mixed separately, then carefully folded with a rubber spatula just until combined.

Creamed muffins have a cake-like texture and require beating the butter and sugar in a mixer until light and fluffy before adding the remaining ingredients.

In every instance, the dry ingredients must be thoroughly combined before the liquid ingredients are added and vice versa. I have found that, in most cases, a medium-size whisk – not a spoon – is the best utensil for mixing the dry ingredients. I use the same whisk to combine the liquid ingredients. The liquid and dry ingredients are then combined with a spatula, or an electric mixer. The most important step in muffin making is to mix the final batter in as few, quick, folding strokes as possible – just until the dry ingredients are moistened – actually a few streaks of flour in the batter is perfectly acceptable. Overmixing produces tough muffins so don't worry if the batter appears lumpy – lumps disappear during baking. Quick breads, on the other hand, often require a little more mixing than muffins to produce a tighter crumb, though quick breads, too, can be overmixed.

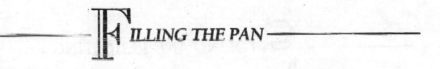

FILLING THE PAN

Most cookbooks advise filling muffin cups two-thirds full. I generally prefer to fill the cups right to the top which produces muffins with high rounded caps.

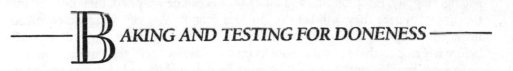

BAKING AND TESTING FOR DONENESS

Use a good oven thermometer to test the temperature of your oven. Every oven has its own idiosyncracies so you may have to adjust cooking times somewhat. Bake muffins or quick breads in the top third of the oven for maximum heat. Always check the muffins or breads at least five minutes before the estimated time to be sure they are not overcooking. To test for doneness, use a wooden skewer or toothpick and insert it into the center of the muffin or bread. If the pick comes out clean, then it is cooked.

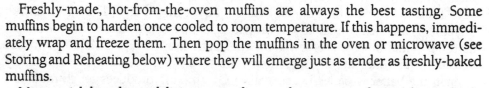

COOLING

Freshly-made, hot-from-the-oven muffins are always the best tasting. Some muffins begin to harden once cooled to room temperature. If this happens, immediately wrap and freeze them. Then pop the muffins in the oven or microwave (see Storing and Reheating below) where they will emerge just as tender as freshly-baked muffins.

Many quick breads are delicious served warm, but most need to cool completely before slicing and serving. Transfer the muffins or breads immediately to a rack to cool for a few minutes, in the case of muffins, or thoroughly for most breads – unless the recipe instructs otherwise.

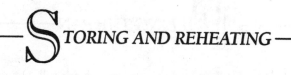

STORING AND REHEATING

The majority of quick breads improve in flavor if wrapped in foil and allowed to stand for 24 hours before slicing. Wrapping in foil also softens the crust for easier slicing. Happily, most muffins and quick breads can be wrapped, then popped into the freezer where they will last for up to a month. You can wrap quick breads unsliced – they stay fresher longer that way – but I prefer to slice my quick breads before freezing so that I can thaw out as many or as few slices at a time as I want.

To store muffins and breads, they must be thoroughly cooled before wrapping.

Wrap cooled muffins and breads in foil or plastic wrap, then place in plastic freezer bags. (Or simply place muffins and breads, unwrapped, in freezer bags.) To thaw muffins, place them, wrapped in foil, in a 350°F oven for 10 minutes or until warmed through. A much superior and quicker method that I learned from my mother: remove wrapping and place an uncovered muffin (only one at a time) in the microwave and cook on high setting for 40 to 50 seconds. Be careful not to overcook or they become hard.

Breads should be thawed at room temperature, still wrapped, or reheated by toasting partially thawed slices in a toaster. Actually, most quick breads make unbelievably delicious toast. Serve at your next breakfast or tea party for a really special treat.

INGREDIENTS

BAKING POWDER: For best results, use "double-acting" baking powder: it reacts once in the batter, then again with oven heat. Be sure your baking powder is fresh. Check the expiration date and replace it if it's past its prime, otherwise your muffins and breads won't rise.

BLACK OLIVES: I use Kalamata olives from Greece in my recipes. You may also use Niçoise olives from France. They are available in specialty food shops and many supermarkets. Canned American olives do not have the flavor or pungency needed for the recipes in this book.

BRAN: Use unprocessed wheat or oat bran which is available at bulk food shops and health food stores. Don't substitute bran cereals for bran in these recipes.

BUTTER: I tested the recipes in this book using lightly salted butter, but you many substitute unsalted if you prefer. I don't recommend margarine – I just don't like the taste of it or the idea of eating a chemically-produced product. Butter is real food and to my logic, better for you. If you disagree, then by all means substitute margarine, but for best results choose a solid margarine, not the ones that stay soft. If you are concerned about animal fats then bake the recipes using vegetable oil, but don't substitute oil in a recipe that calls for butter: it could throw off the liquid balance.

CORIANDER: A pungently aromatic herb also known as cilantro or Chinese parsley. It's available in Asian and Latin American food shops, some supermarkets, and produce stores.

DRIED HERBS: The fresher the dried herbs, the more flavorful your food. Bottled herbs that have lost their color and aroma should be replaced.

FLOUR: I tested recipes using all-purpose flour: it's more readily available, though I prefer unbleached flour which gives a lighter texture to baked goods. Substitute it for all-purpose flour if available. When using whole wheat flour, stone-ground is preferable: it's not only more nutritious but more flavorful, too. Do not substitute "self-rising flour" for all-purpose flour: salt and leavening have been added. The recipes call for unsifted flour unless the recipe suggests otherwise.

GARLIC: It is hard to imagine anyone not cooking with garlic (lots of it!), for it is a seasoning that goes with almost every savory dish. Choose large bulbs that are tightly closed and not sprouting. Squeeze the bulb to make sure it is firm and fresh. Powdered garlic should be avoided in any recipe calling for fresh garlic though it is perfectly acceptable when used with other dried herbs in seasoning mixes for "dry" marinades.

NUTS: To toast nuts, place them on a baking sheet with sides and bake at 350°F until golden brown, watching carefully that they don't burn.

PARMESAN: Be sure to purchase Parmesan that has the words "Parmigiano Reggiano" or second best, "Grana Padano" stamped on the rind. Always grate it fresh just before using: it begins to lose flavor after grating. It is available in Italian food shops or well-stocked cheese stores

SHIITAKE MUSHROOMS: Fresh shiitake mushrooms are now available in many specialty and produce stores – at one time they were only available dried. Shiitake mushrooms are umbrella-shaped, brownish-black in color, with a wonderful earthy flavor.

SUN-DRIED TOMATOES: Salty, with an intense flavor of tomatoes, the best ones are imported from Italy – though there are some quality domestic varieties. Sun-dried tomatoes are available in most specialty and Italian food stores. They are available dry-packed or in oil, in jars. Dry-packed should be aromatic and somewhat pliable – not hard and brown – and reddish colored. Before use, place dry-packed tomatoes in a footed strainer and pour boiling water over to soften them. Pack in sterilized jars and cover with olive oil. You may also add a garlic clove, some oregano, and black peppercorns for added flavor. Store in the refrigerator, but bring back to room temperature before using.

SUGAR: Sugar means granulated white unless otherwise specified. Care should be taken to remove lumps when using brown sugar. When combining dry ingredients, use your fingers to crush the lumps as you are mixing.

VANILLA: Always use pure vanilla

VEGETABLE OIL: I prefer canola oil for baking and cooking, but you may use corn oil if you like or mild-tasting olive oil in savory breads and muffins.

ZEST: The colored outer layer of skin on a citrus fruit.

mixing bowl

S WEE T

M U F F I N S

◆ ◆ ◆

Light muffins with a sweet surprise of marmalade in the center. Be sure to purchase the best quality marmalade – cheaper brands are often too sweet. ◆ *They are just as wonderful filled with strawberry or raspberry jam.*

MARMALADE MUFFINS

2 cups all-purpose flour
¼ cup sugar
1 tablespoon baking
  powder
½ teaspoon salt
2 large eggs
1 cup buttermilk

¼ cup (2 ounces/½ stick)
  butter, melted
1 teaspoon vanilla
Grated zest of 1
  medium-large orange
⅓ cup orange or grapefruit
  marmalade

ADJUST OVEN RACK to top third position; preheat oven to 400°F. Coat 12-cup muffin pan with vegetable spray.

Thoroughly mix flour, sugar, baking powder, and salt in large bowl. In medium bowl, whisk eggs, buttermilk, butter, vanilla, and orange zest until blended. Pour liquid mixture over dry ingredients and fold in with rubber spatula just until combined; do not overmix.

Fill muffin cups a little less than ½ full with batter. With finger, make small indentation in middle of each one and fill with about 1 teaspoon of marmalade. Top up each one with remaining batter – marmalade doesn't have to be completely covered. Bake for 20 minutes or until golden. Turn out onto rack and allow to cool a little before serving. Makes 12 muffins.

BLUEBERRY CORNMEAL MUFFINS

1½ cups all-purpose flour
½ cup yellow cornmeal
⅓ cup sugar
1 tablespoon baking powder
½ teaspoon baking soda
¼ teaspoon salt
1¼ cups sour cream
2 large eggs
¼ cup (2 ounces/½ stick) butter, melted
1½ cups fresh blueberries

ADJUST OVEN RACK to top third position; preheat oven to 400°F. Coat 12-cup muffin pan with vegetable spray.

Thoroughly mix flour, cornmeal, sugar, baking powder, baking soda, and salt in large bowl.

In medium bowl, whisk sour cream, eggs, and butter until blended. Pour liquid mixture over dry ingredients and add blueberries. Fold in with rubber spatula just until combined; do not overmix.

Spoon batter into prepared muffin cups, dividing it evenly. Bake for 20 minutes or until tester comes out clean. Turn out onto rack and serve warm. Makes 12 muffins.

Cornmeal muffins are most often teamed with savory ingredients such as cheese or jalapeños. These delightful muffins are slightly sweet and studded with blueberries.

F resh rhubarb-filled muffins are a delicious taste of early summer, though you can use frozen rhubarb to cook these any time of the year. ♦ If using frozen rhubarb, partially thaw, then dice.

CINNAMON RHUBARB MUFFINS

2 cups all-purpose flour
½ cup sugar
1 tablespoon baking powder
½ teaspoon baking soda
½ teaspoon salt
¼ teaspoon ground cinnamon
2 large eggs

1 cup milk
¼ cup (2 ounces/½ stick) butter, melted
1½ cups diced rhubarb
2 teaspoons vanilla
3 tablespoons sugar mixed with ½ teaspoon ground cinnamon

ADJUST OVEN RACK to top third position; preheat oven to 400°F. Coat 12-cup muffin pan with vegetable spray.

Thoroughly mix flour, sugar, baking powder, baking soda, salt, and cinnamon in large bowl. In medium bowl, whisk eggs, milk, and butter. Stir in rhubarb and vanilla. Pour liquid mixture over dry ingredients and fold in with rubber spatula just until combined; do not overmix.

Spoon batter into prepared muffin cups, dividing it evenly. Sprinkle cinnamon-sugar mixture evenly over muffin tops. Bake for 20 minutes or until tester comes out clean. Turn out onto rack and serve warm. Makes 12 muffins.

GRANNY SMITH APPLE MUFFINS

2 cups all-purpose flour
½ cup packed brown sugar
1 tablespoon baking
   powder
½ teaspoon salt
1½ cups peeled, diced
   (¼-inch pieces), Granny
   Smith apples

2 large eggs
1 cup buttermilk
¼ cup (2 ounces/½ stick)
   butter, melted
½ teaspoon vanilla
3 tablespoons sugar mixed
   with ½ teaspoon ground
   cinnamon

ADJUST OVEN RACK to top third position; preheat oven to 400°F. Coat 12-cup muffin pan with vegetable spray.

Thoroughly mix flour, brown sugar, baking powder, and salt in large bowl; stir in apples. In medium bowl, whisk eggs, buttermilk, butter, and vanilla until blended. Pour liquid mixture over dry ingredients and fold in with rubber spatula just until combined; do not overmix.

Spoon batter into prepared cups, dividing it evenly. Sprinkle cinnamon-sugar mixture evenly over muffin tops. Bake for 20 minutes or until tester comes out clean. Turn out onto rack and serve at room temperature. Makes 12 muffins.

M oist, apple-filled muffins with a spicy cinnamon topping are a tasty nibble. ♦ These muffins must cool to room temperature before serving for best flavor. ♦ Dice the apple into small pieces: large chunks won't be cooked by the time the muffins are ready.

*hese pretty-in-pink muffins
are so delicately seasoned,
it's imperative you use fresh
and very flavorful pink or red
grapefruit – some can be quite tasteless.
♦ Serve with butter and grapefruit marmalade, if desired. ♦ The muffins are best
when allowed to cool a little.*

Pink Grapefruit Muffins

1 large pink or red
  grapefruit, peeled and
  segmented
¼ teaspoon baking soda
½ cup (4 ounces/1 stick)
  butter, at room
  temperature

½ cup sugar
1 large egg
2½ cups all-purpose flour
1 tablespoon baking
  powder
1 teaspoon salt

ADJUST OVEN RACK to top third position; preheat oven to
400°F. Coat 12-cup muffin pan with cooking spray.

Holding grapefruit segments over medium bowl to catch
juices, seed and peel off and discard the bitter white pith
and as much membrane as will come off easily; place in
bowl as completed. Coarsely chop grapefruit with juice in
food processor and return to bowl; stir in baking soda.

Cream butter and sugar in large bowl of electric mixer for
3 minutes or until light and fluffy. Beat in egg.

In medium bowl, thoroughly mix flour, baking powder,
and salt. On low speed, blend in dry ingredients and grapefruit mixture just until combined; do not overmix.

Spoon batter into prepared muffin cups, dividing it
evenly. Bake for 20 minutes or until golden. Turn out onto
rack and serve warm. Makes 12 muffins.

WHOLE ORANGE MUFFINS

2½ cups all-purpose flour
¾ cup sugar
1 tablespoon baking
  powder
1 teaspoon baking soda
¼ teaspoon salt
1 thin-skinned medium
  orange, cut into wedges
  (8ths), and seeds removed

1 large egg
1 cup milk
¼ cup vegetable oil

ADJUST OVEN RACK to top third position; preheat oven to 400°F. Coat 12-cup muffin pan with vegetable spray, including top edges: muffins rise above pan.

Thoroughly combine flour, sugar, baking powder, baking soda, and salt in large bowl.

Purée orange in food processor and transfer to medium bowl. Whisk in egg, milk, and oil until blended then pour over dry ingredients. Fold in with rubber spatula just until combined; do not overmix.

Spoon batter into prepared muffin cups, dividing it evenly. Bake for 20 minutes or until golden. Turn out onto rack and serve warm. Makes 12 muffins.

One day I thought, why not throw in the whole orange and see what happens? Turns out it was an inspired notion with memorable results!

Delicate-textured muffins, fragrant with mango, perfect for nibbling on a sunny afternoon, accompanied by hot or iced tea.

MANGO MUFFINS

2 cups all-purpose flour
1 tablespoon baking powder
½ teaspoon baking soda
½ teaspoon salt
½ cup (4 ounces/1 stick) butter, at room temperature
¾ cup sugar
2 large eggs
Grated zest of 1 large orange
1 cup puréed mango (about 2 large)

ADJUST OVEN RACK to top third position; preheat oven to 400°F. Coat 12-cup muffin pan with vegetable spray.

Thoroughly mix flour, baking powder, baking soda, and salt in medium bowl.

Cream butter and sugar in large bowl of electric mixer for 3 minutes or until light and fluffy. Beat in eggs, one at a time, then orange zest. On low speed, blend in mango and dry ingredients just until combined; do not overmix.

Spoon batter into prepared muffin cups, dividing it evenly. Bake for 20 minutes or until tester comes out clean. Turn out onto rack and serve warm. Makes 12 muffins.

LEMON POPPY SEED MUFFINS

2 cups all-purpose flour	2 large eggs
¾ cup sugar	1 cup buttermilk
¼ cup poppy seeds	¼ cup vegetable oil
1 tablespoon baking powder	Grated zest of 1 medium lemon
1 teaspoon baking soda	⅓ cup fresh lemon juice
½ teaspoon salt	3 tablespoons sugar

ADJUST OVEN RACK to top third position; preheat oven to 400°F. Coat 12-cup muffin pan with vegetable spray.

Thoroughly mix flour, sugar, poppy seeds, baking powder, baking soda, and salt in large bowl. In medium bowl, whisk eggs, buttermilk, oil, and lemon zest until blended. Pour liquid mixture over dry ingredients and fold in with rubber spatula just until combined; do not overmix.

Spoon batter into prepared muffin cups, dividing it evenly. Bake for 20 minutes or until tester comes out clean.

Meanwhile, stir lemon juice and sugar in small bowl until sugar is dissolved; set aside.

When muffins are removed from oven, pierce tops in several places with toothpick. Restir lemon glaze, then slowly drizzle about 1 tablespoon of lemon mixture over each muffin. Allow muffins to cool in pan for 10 minutes to absorb syrup, then remove to rack to cool. Makes 12 muffins.

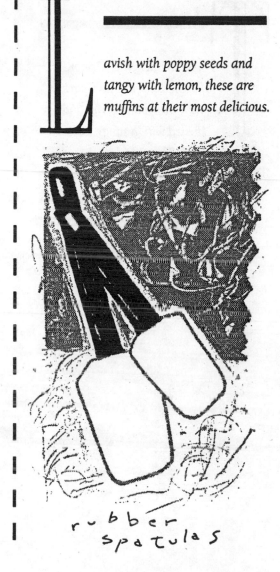

L avish with poppy seeds and tangy with lemon, these are muffins at their most delicious.

rubber spatulas

These are delicately lemon-flavored muffins jam-packed with fresh blueberries and dusted with a tangy lemon-sugar topping. ◆ They are dense muffins, best served fresh from the oven.

BLUEBERRY STREUSEL MUFFINS

2 cups all-purpose flour
1 tablespoon baking powder
½ teaspoon salt
½ teaspoon ground cinnamon
2 cups blueberries
½ cup (4 ounces/1 stick) butter

1 cup sugar
2 large eggs
1 cup milk
Grated zest of 1 medium lemon
¼ cup sugar mixed with finely grated zest of 1 medium lemon

ADJUST OVEN RACK to top third position; preheat oven to 400°F. Coat 12-cup muffin pan with vegetable spray, including top edges: muffins rise above pan.

Thoroughly mix flour, baking powder, salt, and cinnamon in medium bowl; stir in blueberries.

Cream butter and sugar in large bowl of electric mixer for 3 minutes or until light and fluffy. Add eggs one at a time, then milk and lemon zest. On low speed, blend in dry ingredients just until combined; do not overmix.

Spoon batter into prepared muffin cups, dividing it evenly. Sprinkle lemon-sugar mixture evenly over muffin tops. Bake for 25 minutes or until tester comes out clean. Turn out onto rack and serve warm. Makes 12 muffins.

MINCEMEAT MUFFINS

2 cups all-purpose flour
1 tablespoon baking
    powder
½ teaspoon baking soda
½ teaspoon salt
1½ cups best-quality
    bottled mincemeat

1 large egg
¼ cup (2 ounces/½ stick)
    butter, melted
1 cup milk

ADJUST OVEN RACK to top third position; preheat oven to 400°F. Coat 12-cup muffin pan with vegetable spray, including top edges: muffins rise above pan.

Thoroughly mix flour, baking powder, baking soda, and salt in large bowl. In medium bowl, blend mincemeat, egg, butter, and milk. Pour liquid mixture over dry ingredients and fold in with rubber spatula just until combined; do not overmix.

Spoon batter into prepared muffin cups, dividing it evenly. Bake for 20 minutes or until tester comes out clean. Turn out onto rack and serve warm. Makes 12 muffins.

My mother looked through her recipe files and found these exceptionally good muffins. ◆ Serve at Christmastime, or anytime during the year.

What fun it is to collect and peruse old recipe booklets. Here's an "antique" I found in a booklet published in 1932, by the National Biscuit Company under the heading "Let's Go Cracker Cooking." It is a unique recipe using ground ginger snaps in place of flour. ♦ These are very intensely flavored so I prefer to bake little miniature muffins. ♦ Grind the ginger snaps in two or three batches in a food processor.

GINGER SNAP MUFFINS

2 cups finely ground ginger
   snaps (about 30 cookies)
1 tablespoon baking
   powder
½ teaspoon salt

2 large eggs
½ cup milk
¼ cup (2 ounces/½ stick)
   butter, melted

ADJUST OVEN RACK to top third position; preheat oven to 400°F. Coat 30-cup miniature muffin pans with vegetable spray.

Thoroughly mix ground ginger snaps, baking powder, and salt in large bowl. In medium bowl, whisk eggs, milk, and butter until blended. Pour liquid mixture over dry ingredients and fold in with rubber spatula just until combined; do not overmix.

Spoon batter into prepared muffin cups, dividing it evenly. Bake for 12 minutes or until tester comes out clean. Turn out onto rack and serve at room temperature. Makes about 30 miniature muffins.

RASPBERRY MUFFINS
WITH NUTTY TOPPING

2 cups all-purpose flour	2 large eggs
1 cup sugar	Finely grated zest of
1 tablespoon baking	1 medium orange
powder	1 cup fresh raspberries
¼ teaspoon ground	⅓ cup chopped pecans
cinnamon	½ cup packed brown sugar
½ teaspoon salt	⅓ cup all-purpose flour
1 cup buttermilk	3 tablespoons butter,
¼ cup vegetable oil	melted

ADJUST OVEN RACK to top third position; preheat oven to 400°F. Coat 12-cup muffin pan with vegetable spray, including top edges: muffins rise above pan.

Thoroughly mix flour, sugar, baking powder, cinnamon, and salt in large bowl. In medium bowl, whisk buttermilk, oil, eggs, and orange zest until blended. Pour liquid mixture over dry ingredients and add raspberries. Fold in with rubber spatula just until combined; do not overmix.

Spoon batter into prepared muffin cups, dividing it evenly.

To make topping, combine nuts, brown sugar, flour, and butter in bowl, then sprinkle evenly over muffin tops. Bake for 20 minutes or until tester comes out clean. Carefully turn out onto rack to cool. Makes 12 muffins.

L ovely, aromatic, raspberry-filled muffins with a crunchy topping are a special breakfast treat. ♦ I only make these with fresh raspberries – frozen just won't do.

These sweet and tangy muffins flavored with pineapple and buttermilk are wonderful served warm with eggs and bacon or sausages and a cup of hot coffee. ◆ It is preferable to use fresh, perfectly-ripe pineapple, but canned will do.

PINEAPPLE MUFFINS

1 cup puréed unsweetened
   pineapple chunks
2 cups all-purpose flour
1 tablespoon baking
   powder
¾ teaspoon baking soda

½ teaspoon salt
½ cup (4 ounces/1 stick)
   butter, at room
   temperature
1 cup sugar
2 large eggs
Scant ¾ cup buttermilk

ADJUST OVEN RACK to top third position; preheat oven to 400°F. Coat 12-cup muffin pan with vegetable spray, including top edges: muffins rise above pan.

Place puréed pineapple in a fine sieve and stir to release most – but not all – of the juices, reserving liquid for another use if desired.

Thoroughly mix flour, baking powder, baking soda, and salt in medium bowl.

Cream butter and sugar in large bowl of electric mixer for 3 minutes or until light and fluffy. Beat in eggs, one at a time. On low speed, blend in dry ingredients, pineapple, and buttermilk just until combined; do not overmix.

Spoon batter into prepared muffin cups, dividing it evenly.Bake for 20 minutes or until golden. Turn out onto rack and serve warm. Makes 12 muffins.

PEANUT BUTTER AND JELLY MUFFINS

2 cups all-purpose flour
2 tablespoons sugar
1 tablespoon baking
  powder
¼ teaspoon salt
2 large eggs
½ cup creamy peanut
  butter

1 cup milk
¼ cup (2 ounces/½ stick)
  butter, melted
½ cup chopped unsalted
  peanuts
About ⅓ cup grape jelly

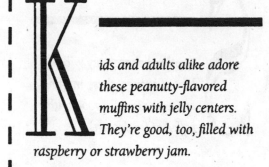

ids and adults alike adore these peanutty-flavored muffins with jelly centers. They're good, too, filled with raspberry or strawberry jam.

ADJUST OVEN RACK to top third position; preheat oven to 400°F. Coat 12-cup muffin pan with vegetable spray.

Thoroughly mix flour, sugar, baking powder, and salt in large bowl. In medium bowl, blend eggs and peanut butter with wooden spoon until smooth. Stir in milk, butter, and peanuts. Pour liquid mixture over dry ingredients and fold in with rubber spatula just until combined; do not overmix.

Fill muffin cups a little less than ½ full with batter. With finger, make small indentation in middle of each one and fill with heaping teaspoon of jelly. Top up each one with remaining batter – jelly doesn't have to be completely covered. Bake for 20 minutes or until golden. Turn out onto rack and allow to cool a little before serving. Serve warm. Makes 12 muffins.

Sweet and chocolatey with a hint of orange, these muffins are exceptionally good with coffee or for dessert.

CHOCOLATE CHIP ORANGE MUFFINS

2 cups all-purpose flour
½ cup sugar
1 tablespoon baking
   powder
½ teaspoon salt
2 large eggs

1 cup milk
¼ cup vegetable oil
Grated zest of 1 medium
   orange
¾ cup chocolate chips

ADJUST OVEN RACK to top third position; preheat oven to 400°F. Coat 12-cup muffin pan with vegetable spray.

Thoroughly mix flour, sugar, baking powder, and salt in large bowl. Whisk eggs, milk, oil, and orange zest in medium bowl until blended. Stir in chocolate chips.

Pour liquid mixture over dry ingredients and fold in with rubber spatula just until combined; do not overmix.

Spoon batter into prepared muffin cups, dividing it evenly. Bake for 20 minutes or until tester comes out clean. Turn out onto rack and serve warm. Makes 12 muffins.

White Chocolate Muffins

¼ cup (2 ounces/½ stick)
   butter, at room
   temperature
2 tablespoons sugar
2 large eggs
Grated zest of 1 large
   orange
½ cup fresh orange juice

½ cup milk
1 tablespoon baking
   powder
½ teaspoon baking soda
2 cups all-purpose flour
½ cup coarsely grated
   white chocolate
¼ cup ground almonds

ADJUST OVEN RACK to top third position; preheat oven to 400°F. Coat 12-cup muffin pan with vegetable spray.

Cream butter and sugar in large bowl of electric mixer for 3 minutes or until light and fluffy. Beat in eggs, one at a time, and orange zest. On low speed, blend in orange juice, milk, baking powder, and baking soda. Fold in flour, chocolate, and almonds with rubber spatula just until combined; do not overmix.

Spoon batter into prepared muffin cups, dividing it evenly. Bake for 15 minutes or until golden. Turn out onto rack and serve warm. Makes 12 muffins.

The perfect indulgence, these chic, subtly-flavored muffins are superb with tea or cups of good espresso, frothy cappucino, or caffe latte. ♦ It is important to coarsely grate the white chocolate – if too fine, the chocolate will blend into the batter and there won't be any tasty chunks of chocolate waiting to surprise and delight!

C hocoholics will adore these superior muffins. Sprinkle the tops with confectioners' sugar if you wish, or omit the sugar to show off their crackly tops. ◆ Add chopped pecans, hazelnuts, or almonds to muffins if desired.

CHOCOLATE INTENSITY MUFFINS

2 cups all-purpose flour
¾ cup unsweetened cocoa
　powder
1¼ cups sugar
1 tablespoon baking
　powder
½ teaspoon baking soda
½ teaspoon salt

2 large eggs
1 cup buttermilk
½ cup (4 ounces/1 stick)
　butter, melted
1 teaspoon vanilla
Confectioners' sugar
　(optional)

ADJUST OVEN RACK to top third position; preheat oven to 400°F. Coat 12-cup muffin pan with vegetable spray, including top edges: muffins rise above pan. (Coat thoroughly: these muffins have a tendency to stick.)

Add flour to large bowl. Sift in cocoa powder. Add sugar, baking powder, baking soda, and salt and thoroughly combine.

Whisk eggs, buttermilk, butter, and vanilla in medium bowl until blended. Pour liquid mixture over dry ingredients and fold in with rubber spatula just until combined; do not overmix.

Spoon batter into prepared muffin cups, dividing it evenly. Bake for 20 minutes or until tester comes out clean. Carefully turn out onto rack. Using tiny sieve, generously dust tops of muffins with confectioners' sugar if desired. Makes 12 muffins.

CHOCOLATE SWIRL MUFFINS

2 ounces semi-sweet
   chocolate
1 teaspoon butter
2 cups all-purpose flour
1 tablespoon baking
   powder
½ teaspoon salt

¼ cup (2 ounces/½ stick)
   butter, at room
   temperature
1 cup sugar
2 large eggs
1¼ cups sour cream
1 teaspoon vanilla

ADJUST OVEN RACK to top third position; preheat oven to 400°F. Coat 12-cup muffin pan with vegetable spray.

Melt chocolate in microwave oven using defrost setting for 1 to 2 minutes or in small saucepan over very low heat. Stir in 1 teaspoon butter and set aside to cool.

Thoroughly mix flour, baking powder, and salt in medium bowl.

Cream butter and sugar in large bowl of electric mixer for 3 minutes or until light and fluffy. Beat in eggs, one at a time, then sour cream and vanilla. Fold in dry ingredients with rubber spatula just until combined; do not overmix. Drizzle in chocolate mixture and carefully draw table knife through batter several times to swirl chocolate.

Carefully spoon batter into prepared muffin cups, dividing it evenly. Using your finger, make a swirl pattern on top of each muffin. Bake for 20 minutes or until tester comes out clean. Turn out onto rack and serve warm. Makes 12 muffins.

Swirling semi-sweet chocolate through the batter is a nice touch, giving these positively scrumptious muffins a pretty ribbon pattern.

veryone's favorite breakfast muffin, these are less cloying than the store-bought variety.

BRAN MUFFINS

2 cups wheat bran
1 cup all-purpose flour
¼ cup packed brown sugar
1 tablespoon baking
  powder
½ teaspoon baking soda
½ teaspoon salt
2 large eggs

1 cup buttermilk
¼ cup (2 ounces/½ stick)
  butter, melted
¼ cup liquid honey
¼ cup molasses
Grated zest of 1 large
  orange
¾ cup currants or raisins

ADJUST OVEN RACK to top third position; preheat oven to 400°F. Coat 12-cup muffin pan with vegetable spray.

Thoroughly mix wheat bran, flour, brown sugar, baking powder, baking soda, and salt in large bowl. Whisk eggs, buttermilk, butter, honey, and molasses in medium bowl until well blended; stir in orange zest and currants or raisins. Pour liquid mixture over dry ingredients and fold in with rubber spatula just until combined; do not overmix.

Spoon batter into prepared muffin cups, dividing it evenly. Bake for 20 minutes or until tester comes out clean. Turn out onto rack and serve warm or at room temperature. Makes 12 muffins.

CRUNCHY GRANOLA MUFFINS

2 cups all-purpose flour
¾ cup granola, lightly
  crushed
¾ cup sugar
1 tablespoon baking
  powder
½ teaspoon baking soda
½ teaspoon salt
2 large eggs
1¼ cups buttermilk
¼ cup (2 ounces/½ stick)
  butter
1 cup coarsely chopped
  pitted prunes

ADJUST OVEN RACK to top third position; preheat oven to 400°F. Coat 12-cup muffin pan with vegetable spray.

Thoroughly mix flour, ½ cup granola, sugar, baking powder, baking soda, and salt in large bowl. Whisk eggs, buttermilk, and butter in medium bowl until blended. Pour liquid mixture over dry ingredients, then add prunes. Fold in mixture with rubber spatula just until combined; do not overmix.

Spoon batter into prepared cups, dividing it evenly. Sprinkle remaining granola evenly over muffin tops. Bake for 20 minutes or until tester comes out clean. Turn out onto rack and allow to cool a little before serving. Makes 12 muffins.

Use really good, not-too-sweet granola – preferably home-made. ◆ These attractive muffins make a splendid accompaniment to a simple breakfast of fresh fruit and yogurt, or any meal for that matter. ◆ To crush the granola, I place it in a plastic freezer or sandwich bag, then lightly crush with a rolling pin – a food processor tends to overprocess.

Old-fashioned gingerbread muffins are good served as a midday treat with coffee or for dessert. ◆ Serve them fresh from the oven: the muffins begin to firm up as they cool.

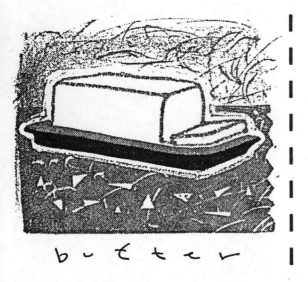

butter

GINGERBREAD MUFFINS WITH HONEY BUTTER

½ cup (4 ounces/1 stick) butter, at room temperature
½ cup brown sugar
2 large eggs
¼ cup molasses
¼ cup liquid honey
2½ cup all-purpose flour
1½ teaspoons baking soda
½ teaspoon salt

1 teaspoon ground cinnamon
1 teaspoon ground ginger
½ teaspoon ground allspice
1 cup boiling water
½ cup raisins
¼ cup liquid honey
¼ cup (2 ounces/½ stick) butter

ADJUST OVEN RACK to top third position; preheat oven to 375°F. Coat 12-cup muffin pan with vegetable spray.

Cream butter and brown sugar in large bowl of electric mixer for 3 minutes or until light and fluffy. Beat in eggs, molasses, and honey until smooth. On low speed, blend in flour, baking soda, salt, cinnamon, ginger, allspice, and boiling water. Stir in raisins.

Spoon batter into prepared muffin cups, dividing it evenly. Bake for 20 minutes or until tester comes out clean. Turn out onto rack and serve hot with Honey Butter if desired.

To make Honey Butter, whisk honey and butter in small bowl until well blended and creamy. Makes 12 large muffins.

CARROT CAKE MUFFINS

1 cup whole wheat flour
1 cup finely ground
   almonds
1 tablespoon baking
   powder
½ teaspoon salt
½ teaspoon ground mace
½ cup packed brown sugar

1 cup lightly packed, finely
   grated carrots
Grated zest of 2 medium
   oranges
2 large eggs
1 cup milk
¼ cup (2 ounces/½ stick)
   butter, melted

ADJUST OVEN RACK to top third position; preheat oven to 400°F. Coat 12-cup muffin pan with vegetable spray.

Thoroughly mix flour, ground almonds, baking powder, salt, and mace in large bowl. With your hands, blend in brown sugar, carrots, and orange zest until no lumps remain. Whisk eggs, milk, and butter in medium bowl. Pour liquid mixture over dry ingredients and fold in with rubber spatula just until combined; do not overmix.

Spoon batter into prepared muffin cups, dividing it evenly. Bake for 20 minutes or until tester comes out clean. Turn out onto rack to cool to room temperature before serving. Makes 12 muffins.

sing ground almonds in place of all-purpose flour gives texture and flavor to these moist muffins.

C hewy and delicious muffins reminiscent of oatmeal cookies, these don't rise as high as typical muffins, but have a unique flat-topped look.

BROWN SUGAR OATMEAL MUFFINS

1¾ cups rolled oats
1 cup all-purpose flour
¼ cup packed brown sugar
2 teaspoons baking powder
½ teaspoon baking soda
½ teaspoon salt
1 large egg

¼ cup (2 ounces / ½ stick)
  butter, melted
1 cup buttermilk
¼ cup honey
1 cup coarsely chopped
  pitted prunes

ADJUST OVEN RACK to top third position; preheat oven to 350°F. Coat 12-cup muffin pan with vegetable spray.

Thoroughly mix oatmeal, flour, brown sugar, baking powder, baking soda, and salt in large bowl. Whisk egg, butter, buttermilk, and honey in medium bowl until well blended; stir in prunes. Pour liquid mixture over dry ingredients and fold in with rubber spatula just until combined; do not overmix.

Spoon batter into prepared muffin cups, dividing it evenly. Bake for 20 minutes or until golden. Turn out onto rack and serve warm or at room temperature. Makes 12 muffins.

PEACH YOGURT MUFFINS

1 ¼ cups all-purpose flour
1 cup rolled oats
¼ cup packed brown sugar
1 tablespoon baking
    powder
½ teaspoon baking soda
¼ teaspoon salt
⅛ teaspoon ground
    cinnamon

2 large eggs
1 cup plain yogurt
¼ cup liquid honey
¼ cup (2 ounces/½ stick)
    butter, melted
1 teaspoon vanilla
1 cup peeled, chopped
    fresh ripe peaches

ADJUST OVEN RACK to top third position; preheat oven to 400°F. Coat 12-cup muffin pan with vegetable spray.

Thoroughly mix flour, oats, brown sugar, baking powder, baking soda, salt, and cinnamon in large bowl. Whisk eggs, yogurt, honey, butter, and vanilla in medium bowl until well blended; stir in peaches. Pour liquid mixture over dry ingredients and fold in with rubber spatula just until combined; do not overmix.

Spoon batter into prepared muffin cups, dividing it evenly. Bake for 20 minutes or until tester comes out clean. Turn out onto rack and serve warm. Makes 12 muffins.

P*eachy keen muffins to serve at breakfast or snack time. Perfectly-ripe, in-season peaches are ideal, of course, but if using canned, be sure to drain them well and place on paper towels to absorb excess liquid before adding.*

O range-colored sweet potato muffins, redolent with pumpkin pie spices, are compatible with Thanksgiving turkey – or ham, goose, or chicken.

SWEET POTATO MUFFINS

2 cups all-purpose flour
1 tablespoon baking
  powder
½ teaspoon salt
¼ teaspoon ground
  cinnamon
¼ teaspoon grated nutmeg
⅛ teaspoon ground ginger
1 cup mashed, cooled
  sweet potato (about
  1 large)

2 large eggs
⅓ cup liquid honey
½ cup milk
¼ cup (2 ounces/½ stick)
  butter, melted
½ cup chopped dates
  or raisins
Grated zest of 1 orange

ADJUST OVEN RACK to top third position; preheat oven to 400°F. Coat 12-cup muffin pan with vegetable spray.

Thoroughly mix flour, baking powder, salt, cinnamon, nutmeg, and ginger in large bowl. Whisk mashed potato, eggs, honey, milk, and butter in medium bowl until well blended; stir in dates and orange zest. Pour liquid mixture over dry ingredients and fold in with rubber spatula just until combined; do not overmix.

Spoon batter into prepared muffin cups, dividing it evenly. Bake for 20 minutes or until tester comes out clean. Turn out onto rack and serve warm. Makes 12 muffins.

UPSIDE DOWN STICKY PECAN MUFFINS

48 pecan halves
½ cup (4 ounces/1 stick) butter, melted
½ cup brown sugar
2 cups all-purpose flour
¼ cup packed brown sugar
1 tablespoon baking powder

½ teaspoon salt
2 large eggs
1 cup buttermilk
¼ cup (2 ounces/½ stick) butter, melted
½ teaspoon vanilla
¼ teaspoon ground cinnamon

ADJUST OVEN RACK to top third position; preheat oven to 400°F. Coat 12-cup nonstick muffin pan with vegetable spray.

Place 4 pecan halves in a single layer in each muffin cup. Spoon about 1 tablespoon each of melted butter and brown sugar on top of nuts.

Thoroughly mix flour, brown sugar, baking powder, and salt in large bowl. Whisk eggs, buttermilk, butter, vanilla, and cinnamon in medium bowl until blended. Pour liquid mixture over dry ingredients and fold in with rubber spatula just until combined; do not overmix.

Spoon batter over brown sugar mixture, dividing it evenly. Bake for 8 minutes, reduce heat to 350°F and bake 12 minutes more or until tester comes out clean. Remove muffin pan from oven, place a large piece of foil over pan and, holding edges of foil, turn it over and place on rack. Lift off pan – muffins will now be standing sticky side up – and allow to cool a little before serving. Makes 12 muffins.

Yeast-risen sticky buns take hours to make; these are just as yummy and take only minutes! ◆ For best results, use a nonstick muffin pan.

G

ood-for-you muffins are packed with whole grain flours, seeds, and nuts. ◆

VIRTUOUS MUFFINS

1½ cups whole wheat flour
¼ cup all-purpose flour
¼ cup buckwheat flour
¼ cup wheat or oat bran
¼ cup dry milk powder
¼ cup wheat germ
¼ cup chopped sunflower
  seeds
¼ cup chopped nuts
¼ cup packed brown sugar
1 tablespoon baking
  powder

¼ teaspoon salt
2 large eggs
1 cup milk
¼ cup vegetable oil
  (preferably canola oil)
½ cup liquid honey
¼ cup chopped dates,
  prunes, or raisins
¼ cup chopped dried
  apricots

ADJUST OVEN RACK to top third position; preheat oven to 400°F. Coat 12-cup muffin pan with vegetable spray.

Thoroughly combine flours, wheat bran, dry milk powder, wheat germ, sunflower seeds, nuts, brown sugar, baking powder, and salt in large bowl. Whisk eggs, milk, oil, and honey in medium bowl; stir in dates and apricots. Pour liquid mixture over dry ingredients and fold in with rubber spatula just until combined; do not overmix.

Spoon batter into prepared muffin cups, dividing it evenly. Bake for 15 minutes or until tester comes out clean. Turn out onto rack and serve warm or at room temperature. Makes 12 muffins.

LIME MUFFINS

2 cups all-purpose flour
1 tablespoon baking
   powder
½ teaspoon salt
½ cup (4 ounces/1 stick)
   butter

¾ cup sugar
2 large eggs
¾ cup frozen limeade
   concentrate, thawed
Grated zest of 1 large lime

ADJUST OVEN RACK to top third position; preheat oven to 400°F. Coat 12-cup muffin pan with vegetable spray. (Coat thoroughly: these muffins have a tendency to stick.)

Thoroughly mix flour, baking powder, and salt in medium bowl.

Cream butter and sugar in large bowl of electric mixer for 3 minutes or until light and fluffy. Beat in eggs, one at a time, then limeade and lime zest. On low speed, blend in dry ingredients just until combined; do not overmix.

Spoon batter into prepared muffin cups, dividing it evenly. Bake for 20 minutes or until tester comes out clean. Turn out onto rack and serve warm. Makes 12 muffins.

crave citrus flavors like chocoholics crave chocolate. That's why I concocted these delightful muffins.

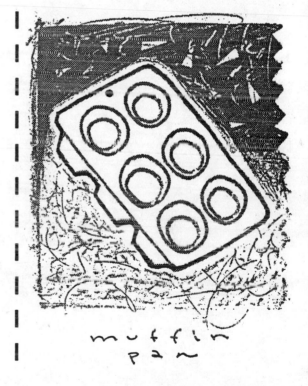

muffin pan

ncredibly moist and delicious muffins that make lovely gifts for family and friends.

BANANA SPICE MUFFINS

2 cups all-purpose flour
1 tablespoon baking
  powder
½ teaspoon salt
¼ teaspoon ground ginger
¼ teaspoon ground
  cinnamon
¼ teaspoon grated nutmeg
½ cup (4 ounces/1 stick)
  butter, at room
  temperature

1 cup sugar
2 large eggs
1 cup milk
1 teaspoon vanilla
2 very ripe bananas,
  mashed but still chunky

ADJUST OVEN RACK to top third position; preheat oven to 400°F. Coat 12-cup muffin pan with vegetable spray, including top edges: muffins rise above pan.

Thoroughly mix flour, baking powder, salt, ginger, cinnamon, and nutmeg in medium bowl.

Cream butter and sugar in large bowl of electric mixer for 3 minutes or until light and fluffy. Beat in eggs one at a time, then milk and vanilla. On low speed blend in dry ingredients and bananas just until combined; do not overmix.

Spoon batter into prepared muffin cups, dividing it evenly. Bake for 25 minutes or until golden and tester comes out clean. Turn out onto rack and serve warm. Makes 12 muffins.

SAVORY MUFFINS

♦ ♦ ♦

erb-flavored, piquant muffins that go well with soup or a savory omelet.

CREAM CHEESE AND CHIVES MUFFINS

2 cups all-purpose flour
1 tablespoon sugar
1 tablespoon baking powder
½ teaspoon baking soda
½ teaspoon salt
¼ teaspoon freshly ground black pepper
5-ounce package herbed cream cheese spread (such as Boursin), at room temperature

2 teaspoons finely chopped fresh chives
2 large eggs
½ cup milk
½ cup sour cream
¼ cup (2 ounces/½ stick) butter, melted

ADJUST OVEN RACK to top third position; preheat oven to 375°F. Generously coat 12-cup muffin pan with vegetable spray.

Thoroughly mix flour, sugar, baking powder, baking soda, salt, and pepper in large bowl. Whisk cream cheese, chives, eggs, and milk in medium bowl until well blended, then whisk in sour cream and butter. Pour liquid mixture over dry ingredients and fold in with rubber spatula just until combined; do not overmix.

Spoon batter into prepared muffin cups, dividing it evenly. Bake for 20 minutes or until tester comes out clean. Turn out onto rack and serve warm. Makes 12 muffins.

EXCEPTIONAL CORNMEAL MUFFINS

1½ cups all-purpose flour
½ cup yellow cornmeal
1 tablespoon baking
  powder
½ teaspoon salt
½ cup (4 ounces/1 stick)
  butter, at room
  temperature

½ cup sugar
2 large eggs
1 cup milk

ADJUST OVEN RACK to top third position; preheat oven to 400°F. Coat 12-cup muffin pan with vegetable spray, including top edges: muffins rise above pan.

Thoroughly mix flour, cornmeal, baking powder, and salt in medium bowl.

Cream butter and sugar in large bowl of electric mixer for 3 minutes or until light and fluffy. Beat in eggs, one at a time, then milk. On low speed, blend in dry ingredients just until combined.

Spoon batter into prepared muffin cups, dividing it evenly. Bake for 20 minutes or until tops are golden. Turn out onto rack and serve hot. Makes 12 muffins.

E*veryone, it seems, is searching for the ultimate cornmeal muffin. ♦ I tested several classic recipes and was totally disappointed with the results: they were mostly dry, heavy, and dull. But then, during Drew's and my winter vacation in Boca Raton, Florida, we dined at one of our favorite local restaurants, Tom's Ribs. I analyzed the texture and taste of their exceptional muffins and realized the secret: a cake-like batter; a delicate cornmeal flavor – obviously a ratio of much more flour to cornmeal – and more sugar.*

Leftover rice is the main ingredient in these simple, unaffected muffins. ♦ This recipe dates all the way back to the early 1900s – I found several renditions of it in old recipe booklets of the era. The best way to describe the flavor and texture is that they're somewhat akin to baking powder biscuits. And just like them, rice muffins have a natural affinity for butter and chunky homemade jam.

RICE MUFFINS

1 cup all-purpose flour
2 teaspoons baking powder
1 teaspoon sugar
½ teaspoon salt
¾ cup milk

¼ cup (2 ounces/½ stick) butter, melted
1 large egg
1 cup cold cooked white rice

ADJUST OVEN RACK to top third position; preheat oven to 400°F. Coat 12-cup muffin pan with vegetable spray.

Thoroughly mix flour, baking powder, sugar, and salt in large bowl. In medium bowl, whisk milk, butter, and egg until blended. Break up rice until free from lumps and stir into milk mixture. Pour liquid mixture over dry ingredients and stir until thoroughly combined.

Spoon batter into prepared muffin cups, dividing it evenly. Bake for 15 minutes or until light golden colored and tester comes out clean. Turn out onto rack and serve hot. Makes 12 muffins.

CHEDDAR MUSTARD MUFFINS

2 cups all-purpose flour
1 tablespoon baking
   powder
1 tablespoon sugar
½ teaspoon salt
Freshly ground black
   pepper
1 cup extra-sharp grated
   Cheddar cheese (about
   4 ounces)
2 large eggs

¾ cup milk
¼ cup (2 ounces/½ stick)
   butter, melted
3 tablespoons Dijon
   mustard
1 green onion (green part
   only), finely chopped
2 tablespoons very finely
   diced sweet red pepper
   (optional)

ADJUST OVEN RACK to top third position; preheat oven to 400°F. Coat 12-cup muffin pan with vegetable spray.

Thoroughly mix flour, baking powder, sugar, salt, and pepper in large bowl. In medium bowl, whisk cheese, eggs, milk, butter, mustard, green onion, and red pepper until blended. Pour liquid mixture over dry ingredients and fold in with rubber spatula just until combined; do not overmix.

Spoon batter into prepared muffin cups, dividing it evenly. Bake for 20 minutes or until golden. Turn out onto rack and serve warm. Makes 12 muffins

A *savory accompaniment to soups, lunches, or a quick snack or lunch in themselves.*

mustard

Blue cheese lover that I am, I couldn't resist adding it to muffin batter. ♦ It makes a marvelous muffin. Serve with fruit: pears, apples, or grapes if you wish.

BLUE CHEESE MUFFINS

2 cups all-purpose flour
3 tablespoons sugar
1 tablespoon baking
  powder
¼ teaspoon salt
2 large eggs

1 cup milk
¼ cup (2 ounces/½ stick)
  butter, melted
1 cup crumbled blue
  cheese

ADJUST OVEN RACK to top third position; preheat oven to 400°F. Coat 12-cup muffin pan with vegetable spray.

Thoroughly mix flour, sugar, baking powder, and salt in large bowl. Whisk eggs, milk, and butter in medium bowl; stir in cheese. Pour liquid mixture over dry ingredients and fold in with rubber spatula just until combined; do not overmix.

Spoon batter into prepared muffin cups, dividing it evenly. Bake for 20 minutes or until tester comes out clean. Turn out onto rack and cool to room temperature before serving. Makes 12 muffins.

WILD RICE AND SHIITAKE MUFFINS

1½ cups chicken stock
¾ cup raw wild rice (or
    1½ cups cold cooked
    wild rice)
¼ cup (2 ounces/½ stick)
    butter
1 small onion, chopped
1 small garlic, chopped
6 ounces fresh shiitake
    mushrooms, stems
    removed and very
    coarsely chopped

1½ cups all-purpose flour
1 tablespoon sugar
1 tablespoon baking
    powder
½ teaspoon salt
2 large eggs
1 cup milk

Earthy, wonderful, these sublime muffins are the perfect accompaniment to a tossed salad; or serve with poultry or game. Or simply enjoy as a delicious savory nibble.

TO COOK RICE, bring chicken stock to a boil in small heavy saucepan. Stir in rice, cover, and simmer for 15 minutes or until liquid is absorbed and rice is tender (adding more liquid if necessary). You should have 1½ cups cooked rice. Set aside to cool completely.

Melt butter in medium nonstick skillet over medium heat. Add onion and garlic and cook for 2 minutes or until tender. Add mushrooms and cook for 2 minutes or until tender; set aside to cool.

Adjust oven rack to top third position; preheat oven to 400°F. Coat 12-cup muffin pan with vegetable spray.

Thoroughly mix flour, sugar, baking powder, and salt in large bowl. Whisk eggs and milk in medium bowl; stir in cooled rice and onion-mushroom mixture until well blended. Pour liquid mixture over dry ingredients and fold in with rubber spatula just until combined; do not overmix.

Spoon batter into prepared muffin cups, dividing it evenly. Bake for 20 minutes or until tester comes out clean. Turn out onto rack and serve warm. Makes 12 muffins.

K

ids love these muffins: when eaten hot, the cheese inside is stringy just like pizza!

PIZZA MUFFINS

2 cups all-purpose flour
1 tablespoon sugar
1 tablespoon baking
  powder
½ teaspoon salt
¼ teaspoon dried oregano
⅛ teaspoon cayenne
2 large eggs
1 cup milk

¼ cup olive oil
1 small garlic clove, minced
1 ripe plum tomato, seeded
  and diced
¼ cup coarsely chopped
  pimiento-stuffed green
  olives
1½ cups cubed mozzarella
  cheese

ADJUST OVEN RACK to top third position; preheat oven to 400°F. Coat 12-cup muffin pan with vegetable spray.

Thoroughly mix flour, sugar, baking powder, salt, oregano, and cayenne in large bowl. Whisk eggs, milk, and olive oil in medium bowl until blended, then stir in garlic, tomato, olives, and cheese. Pour liquid mixture over dry ingredients and fold in with rubber spatula just until combined; do not overmix.

Spoon batter into prepared muffin cups, dividing it evenly. Bake for 20 minutes or until tester comes out clean. Turn out onto rack and serve at once. Makes 12 muffins.

SWEET

QUICK BREADS

♦ ♦ ♦

F *lecked with colorful candied fruits and cherries and dusted with confectioners' sugar, this is a festive bread to serve during the holiday season.*

TUTTI FRUTTI BREAD

2 cups all-purpose flour
2 teaspoons baking powder
½ teaspoon baking soda
½ teaspoon salt
2 large eggs
1 cup milk
½ cup liquid honey
¼ cup (2 ounces/½ stick)
   butter, melted

1 cup candied fruits
   (orange and lemon zest)
½ cup candied red cherries
Grated zest of 1 large
   orange
Confectioners' sugar

ADJUST OVEN RACK to top third position; preheat oven to 350°F. Coat 9 x 5 x 3-inch loaf pan with vegetable spray.

Thoroughly mix flour, baking powder, baking soda, and salt in large bowl. Whisk eggs, milk, honey, and butter in medium bowl until well blended; stir in candied fruits, cherries, and orange zest. Pour liquid mixture over dry ingredients and fold in with rubber spatula just until combined; do not overmix.

Spoon batter into prepared pan, smoothing it on top. Bake for 1 hour or until tester comes out clean. Turn out onto rack and, using a tiny sieve, generously dust top with confectioners' sugar. Allow to cool completely before slicing. Makes 1 loaf.

THREE BERRY BREAD

2 cups all-purpose flour
¾ cup sugar
2 teaspoons baking powder
½ teaspoon baking soda
½ teaspoon salt
2 large eggs
1 cup buttermilk
½ cup (4 ounces/1 stick)
   butter, melted

1 cup fresh raspberries
½ cup diced fresh
   strawberries
½ cup blueberries, fresh
   or frozen
Grated zest of 1 large
   orange

ADJUST OVEN RACK to top third position; preheat oven to 350°F. Coat 9 x 5 x 3-inch loaf pan with vegetable spray.

Thoroughly mix flour, sugar, baking powder, baking soda, and salt in large bowl. Whisk eggs, buttermilk, and butter in medium bowl; stir in berries and orange zest. Pour liquid mixture over dry ingredients and fold in with rubber spatula just until combined, do not overmix.

Spoon batter into prepared pan, smoothing it on top. Bake for 1 hour or until tester comes out clean. Turn out onto rack and cool before slicing. Makes 1 loaf.

B

e sure to use fresh, ripe – not frozen – raspberries and strawberries, though frozen blueberries are fine.

H*appily, fresh pears are available year-round. Here they combine with hazelnuts (also called filberts) in a lovely* bread that's just right with a spot of tea or a late night espresso.

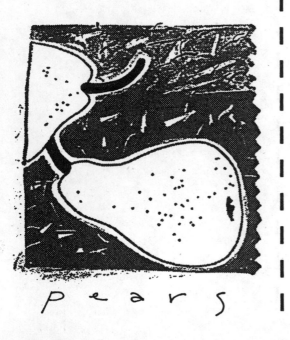

pears

PEAR HAZELNUT BREAD

2 cups all-purpose flour
⅓ cup finely chopped
   toasted hazelnuts
¾ cup sugar
2 teaspoons baking powder
½ teaspoon baking soda
½ teaspoon salt
¼ teaspoon ground
   cinnamon

2 large eggs
¾ cup plain yogurt
½ cup (4 ounces/1 stick)
   butter, melted
Grated zest of 1 medium
   lemon
1½ cups peeled, diced
   (¼-inch pieces) ripe
   pears (about 2 medium)

ADJUST OVEN RACK to top third position; preheat oven to 350°F. Coat 9 x 5 x 3-inch loaf pan with vegetable spray.

   Thoroughly mix flour, hazelnuts, sugar, baking powder, baking soda, salt, and cinnamon in large bowl. Whisk eggs, yogurt, butter, and lemon zest in medium bowl; stir in pears. Pour liquid mixture over dry ingredients and fold in with rubber spatula just until combined; do not overmix.

   Spoon batter into prepared pan; smoothing it on top. Bake for 1 hour or until tester comes out clean. Turn out onto rack and cool completely before slicing. Makes 1 loaf.

RUM RAISIN BREAD

½ cup dark rum
1 teaspoon vanilla
½ cup golden raisins
½ cup currants
Grated zest of 1 large lemon
2 cups all-purpose flour
¾ cup sugar
2 teaspoons baking powder

½ teaspoon baking soda
½ teaspoon salt
¼ teaspoon grated nutmeg
2 large eggs
½ cup sour cream
¼ cup (2 ounces/½ stick)
   butter, melted
Confectioners' sugar

COMBINE RUM, vanilla, raisins, currants, and lemon zest in medium bowl, allow to stand 30 minutes.

Adjust oven rack to top third position; preheat oven to 350°F. Coat 9 x 5 x 3-inch loaf pan with vegetable spray.

Thoroughly mix flour, sugar, baking powder, baking soda, salt, and nutmeg in large bowl.

Stir eggs, sour cream, and butter into rum mixture until well blended. Pour liquid mixture over dry ingredients and fold in with rubber spatula just until combined; do not overmix.

Spoon batter into prepared pan, smoothing it on top. Bake for 1 hour to 1 hour and 15 minutes or until tester comes out clean. Turn out onto rack and, using a tiny sieve, generously dust top with confectioners' sugar. Allow to cool before slicing. Makes 1 loaf.

For me, just stirring this aromatic rummy-raisin batter conjures up delicious Christmas memories — though this is definitely a bread for all seasons. ◆ Actually, I bake this bread for only one reason: it makes unbelievably delicious toast to serve at breakfast-time!

Sweet and delicate-tasting, this old-fashioned tea bread is, of course, just right with a cup of tea – and toasted, too. ♦ *Prepare it with a wild-flower honey which adds lovely fragrance.*

MILK AND HONEY BREAD

1 cup milk	2 teaspoons baking powder
⅔ cup fragrant honey	1 teaspoon salt
¼ cup (2 ounces/½ stick) butter	2 large eggs
2½ cups all-purpose flour	½ cup chopped pistachios or pecans

ADJUST OVEN RACK to top third position; preheat oven to 350°F. Coat 9 x 5 x 3-inch loaf pan with vegetable spray.

Heat milk, honey, and butter in medium saucepan until honey is dissolved; set aside to cool.

Thoroughly mix flour, baking powder, and salt in large bowl. Whisk eggs into cooled milk mixture until blended. Pour liquid mixture over dry ingredients, add pistachios, and fold in with rubber spatula just until combined; do not overmix.

Spoon batter into prepared pan, smoothing it on top. Bake for 50 minutes or until tester comes out clean. Turn out onto rack and allow to cool. Makes 1 loaf.

TRIPLE CHOCOLATE BREAD

5 ounces semisweet
   chocolate
2 ounces unsweetened
   chocolate
¼ cup (2 ounces/½ stick)
   butter
2 cups all-purpose flour
¾ cup sugar

2 teaspoons baking powder
½ teaspoon baking soda
½ teaspoon salt
2 large eggs
¾ cup buttermilk
1 teaspoon vanilla
1 cup white chocolate
   chips

ADJUST OVEN RACK to top third position; preheat oven to
350°F. Coat 9 x 5 x 3-inch loaf pan with vegetable spray.
   Melt chocolate and butter in microwave oven using
defrost setting for 1 to 2 minutes or in small saucepan over
very low heat; set aside to cool.
   Thoroughly mix flour, sugar, baking powder, baking
soda, and salt in large bowl. Whisk eggs, buttermilk, vanilla,
and chocolate mixture in medium bowl until well blended.
Pour liquid mixture over dry ingredients and add white
chocolate chips; fold in with rubber spatula just until combined; do not overmix.
   Spoon batter into prepared pan, smoothing it on top.
Bake for 1 hour or until tester comes out clean. Carefully
turn out onto rack to cool before slicing. Makes 1 loaf.

R*ich and chocolatey, this bread will delight the most discriminating chocolate fanatic.*

Perfumed with the scent of rose, this exotic bread is lovely served in the garden on a gorgeous summer's day. ♦ To make rose water, purchase essence of rose from a pharmacist, then dilute according to their instructions, or purchase rose water from a specialty food shop. ♦ Don't use roses from florists that have been sprayed with chemicals: pick them from your own organic garden or purchase from a gourmet food supplier – ask for edible roses. The rose petals must be highly-scented red roses to give fragrance to the bread.

ROSE PETAL BREAD

2 cups all-purpose flour
2 teaspoons baking powder
½ teaspoon salt
½ cup (4 ounces/1 stick) butter, at room temperature
¾ cup sugar
2 large eggs

1 teaspoon rose water
Grated zest of 1 large orange
1 cup milk
½ cup red rose petals, white part trimmed, and torn into pieces
Confectioners' sugar

ADJUST OVEN RACK to top third position; preheat oven to 350°F. Coat 9 x 5 x 3-inch loaf pan with vegetable spray.

Thoroughly mix flour, baking powder, and salt in medium bowl.

Cream butter and sugar in large bowl of electric mixer for 3 minutes or until light and fluffy. Beat in eggs, one at a time, then rose water and orange zest. On low speed, blend in dry ingredients and milk just until combined; do not overmix. fold in rose petals.

Spoon batter into prepared loaf pan, smoothing it on top. Bake for 1 hour or until tester comes out clean. Turn out onto rack, dust with confectioners' sugar, and cool completely before slicing. Makes 1 loaf.

PEANUT BUTTER AND CHOCOLATE CHIP BREAD

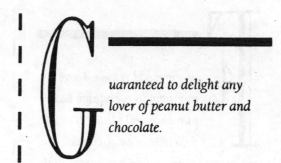

uaranteed to delight any lover of peanut butter and chocolate.

2 cups all-purpose flour
2 teaspoons baking powder
½ teaspoon baking soda
½ teaspoon salt
¾ cup chunky peanut
    butter
½ cup sugar

¼ cup (2 ounces/½ stick)
    butter, at room
    temperature
2 large eggs
1 cup buttermilk
1 cup chocolate chips

ADJUST OVEN RACK to top third position; preheat oven to 350°F. Coat 9 x 5 x 3-inch loaf pan with vegetable spray.

Thoroughly mix flour, baking powder, baking soda, and salt in medium bowl.

Cream peanut butter, sugar, and butter in large bowl of electric mixer for 3 minutes or until well combined. Beat in eggs, one at a time, then buttermilk. On low speed, blend in dry ingredients just until combined. Fold in chocolate chips.

Spoon batter into prepared pan, smoothing it on top. Bake for 50 minutes or until tester comes out clean. Carefully turn out onto rack to cool before slicing. Makes 1 loaf.

For some odd reason, I love pumpkin in everything but pumpkin pie! I think it's delicious in soup, cookies, pickles, ice cream, made into candy, and in this moist, vibrant-colored loaf. ◆ Serve the bread warm, with butter, and a pot of tea. ◆ This recipe is reprinted from my book Joie Warner's Quebec Country Cooking.

PUMPKIN BREAD

2 cups all-purpose flour
2 teaspoons baking powder
½ teaspoon baking soda
½ teaspoon salt
1 cup packed brown sugar
1 teaspoon ground cinnamon
½ teaspoon grated nutmeg
½ teaspoon ground cloves

2 large eggs
½ cup (4 ounces/1 stick) butter, melted
⅓ cup pure maple syrup
1 cup puréed fresh steamed pumpkin, or canned unsweetened
½ cup golden raisins

ADJUST OVEN RACK to top third position; preheat oven to 375°F. Coat 9 x 5 x 3-inch loaf pan with vegetable spray.

Thoroughly mix flour, baking powder, baking soda, salt, brown sugar, cinnamon, nutmeg, and cloves in large bowl.

Whisk eggs, butter, maple syrup, and pumpkin purée in medium bowl until blended, then stir in raisins. Pour liquid mixture over dry ingredients and fold in with rubber spatula just until combined; do not overmix.

Spoon batter into prepared pan, smoothing it on top. Bake for 45 minutes or until tester comes out clean. Carefully turn out onto rack and serve warm or at room temperature. Makes 1 loaf.

ORANGE BLUEBERRY BREAD

1½ cups all-purpose flour
2 teaspoons baking powder
½ teaspoon salt
½ cup (4 ounces/1 stick) butter, at room temperature
¾ cup sugar
2 large eggs

Grated zest of 1 large orange
½ cup fresh orange juice
1 tablespoon vanilla
1 cup blueberries
⅓ cup fresh orange juice
⅓ cup sugar

ADJUST OVEN RACK to top third position; preheat oven to 350°F. Coat 9 x 5 x 3-inch loaf pan with vegetable spray.

Thoroughly mix flour, baking powder, and salt in medium bowl.

Cream butter and sugar in large bowl of electric mixer for 3 minutes or until light and fluffy. Beat in eggs, one at a time, then orange zest, orange juice, and vanilla. On low speed, blend in dry ingredients for only a few seconds or until not quite combined. Fold in blueberries with rubber spatula just until combined; do not overmix.

Spoon batter into prepared pan, smoothing it on top. Bake for 1 hour or until tester comes out clean.

Meanwhile, stir orange juice and sugar until sugar is dissolved. When bread is removed from oven, pierce top in several places with toothpick. Restir orange glaze and slowly drizzle over bread. Allow to cool in pan for 20 minutes. Turn out onto rack and serve warm or at room temperature. Makes 1 loaf.

A super moist, flavorful bread that is wonderful to make for gift giving. ◆ This is my version of my friend Sue Calden's recipe that she serves at The Pink House, a charming bed-and-breakfast in East Hampton, New York.

I am particularly fond of this moist, tangy bread and think it's terrific with a cup of tea.

♦ As a variation, I often add a cup of fresh blueberries, stirring them into the batter just before spooning it into the loaf pan.

LEMON BREAD WITH LEMON GLAZE

1½ cups all-purpose flour
1 teaspoon baking powder
¼ teaspoon salt
6 tablespoons (¾ stick) butter, at room temperature
1 cup sugar
2 large eggs

Grated zest of 1 medium lemon
½ cup buttermilk
¼ cup fresh lemon juice
⅓ cup sugar
Grated zest of 1 medium lemon

ADJUST OVEN RACK to top third position; preheat oven to 350°F. Coat 9 x 5 x 3-inch loaf pan with vegetable spray.

Thoroughly mix flour, baking powder, and salt in medium bowl. Cream butter and sugar in large bowl of electric mixer for 3 minutes or until light and fluffy. Beat in eggs, one at a time, then lemon zest and buttermilk. On low speed, blend in dry ingredients just until combined; do not overmix.

Spoon batter into prepared pan, smoothing it on top. Bake for 1 hour or until tester comes out clean.

Meanwhile, stir lemon juice and sugar in bowl until sugar is dissolved. When bread is removed from oven, immediately turn out onto large piece of foil and pierce top in several places with toothpick. Restir lemon glaze mixture and slowly drizzle over bread. Sprinkle top with grated zest and cool completely before slicing. Makes 1 loaf.

PINK LEMONADE BREAD

¾ cup frozen pink lemonade concentrate, thawed
¼ cup liquid honey
2 cups all-purpose flour
1 tablespoon baking powder
½ teaspoon salt
½ cup (4 ounces/1 stick) butter, at room temperature
½ cup sugar
2 large eggs
Grated zest of 1 large lemon
Confectioners' sugar

ADJUST OVEN RACK to top third position; preheat oven to 350°F. Coat 9 x 5 x 3-inch loaf pan with vegetable spray.

Heat lemonade and honey in small saucepan until honey is dissolved; set aside to cool.

Thoroughly mix flour, baking powder, and salt in medium bowl.

Cream butter and sugar in large bowl of electric mixer for 3 minutes or until light and fluffy. Beat in eggs, one at a time, then lemon zest and cooled lemonade mixture. On low speed, blend in dry ingredients just until combined; do not overmix.

Spoon batter into prepared pan, smoothing it on top. Bake for 50 minutes or until tester comes out clean. Turn out onto rack and, using a tiny sieve, generously dust top with confectioners' sugar. Cool completely before slicing. Makes 1 loaf.

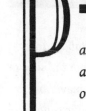

Pastel-pink lemonade bread is a treasure befitting gift-giving or afternoon tea.

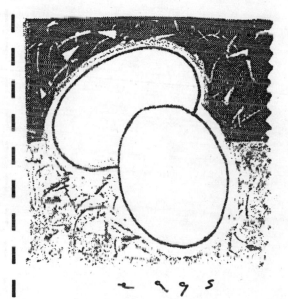

eggs

*favorite of vegetable garden-
ers, this is a wonderful way to
profit from that inevitable
profusion of prolific squash.*

ZUCCHINI PECAN BREAD

1½ cups all-purpose flour
¾ cup sugar
1 tablespoon baking
  powder
½ teaspoon baking soda
½ teaspoon salt
½ teaspoon ground
  cinnamon

2 large eggs
½ cup vegetable oil
1½ cups lightly packed
  shredded unpeeled
  zucchini
½ cup chopped pecans
Grated zest of 1 large
  orange

ADJUST OVEN RACK to top third position; preheat oven to
350°F. Coat 9 x 5 x 3-inch loaf pan with vegetable spray.

Thoroughly mix flour, sugar, baking powder, baking
soda, salt, and cinnamon in large bowl. In medium bowl,
whisk eggs and oil, then stir in zucchini, pecans, and
orange zest.

Pour liquid mixture over dry ingredients and stir with
wooden spoon until well combined – it's a stiff batter.

Spoon battér into prepared pan, smoothing it on top.
Bake for 50 minutes or until tester comes out clean. Care-
fully turn out onto rack to cool completely. Wrap in foil.
Makes 1 loaf.

TOASTED COCONUT BREAD

1 cup shredded sweetened
   coconut
2 cups all-purpose flour
¾ cup sugar
2 teaspoons baking powder
½ teaspoon salt

1 large egg
1 cup milk
¼ cup (2 ounces/½ stick)
   butter, melted
1 teaspoon vanilla

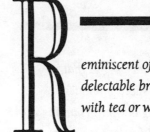

Reminiscent of macaroons, this delectable bread is wonderful with tea or with curry dinners.

ADJUST OVEN RACK to top third position; preheat oven to 350°F. Coat 9 x 5 x 3-inch loaf pan with vegetable spray.

Toast coconut, stirring constantly, in a small ungreased nonstick skillet over medium-high heat, being careful not to let it burn. Let stand until cool.

Thoroughly mix flour, sugar, baking powder, salt, and coconut in large bowl. In medium bowl, whisk egg, milk, butter, and vanilla until blended. Pour liquid mixture over dry ingredients and fold in with rubber spatula just until combined; do not overmix.

Spoon batter into prepared pan, smoothing it on top. Bake for 1 hour or until tester comes out clean. Turn out onto rack to cool completely before slicing. Makes 1 loaf.

An aromatic bread that is lovely sliced into thick rectangular fingers and served for dessert with a selection of cheeses and fresh fruit. Or serve the bread sliced, toasted, and buttered accompanied by cheese for a mid-afternoon snack. ♦ Walnuts, of course, can be substituted for the pecans.

PECAN BREAD

2 cups all-purpose flour
¾ cup packed brown sugar
2 teaspoons baking powder
½ teaspoon salt
½ teaspoon ground cinnamon
½ teaspoon ground ginger
½ teaspoon ground nutmeg

1 cup milk
2 large eggs
½ teaspoon vanilla
¼ cup (2 ounces/½ stick) butter, melted
½ cup pecan halves, broken into large pieces

ADJUST OVEN RACK to top third position; preheat oven to 350°F. Coat 9 x 5 x 3-inch loaf pan with vegetable spray.

Thoroughly mix flour, brown sugar, baking powder, salt, cinnamon, ginger, and nutmeg in large bowl. Whisk milk, eggs, vanilla, and butter in medium bowl until blended; stir in pecans. Pour liquid mixture over dry ingredients and fold in with rubber spatula just until combined; do not overmix.

Spoon batter into prepared pan, smoothing it on top. Bake for 50 minutes or until tester comes out clean. Carefully turn out onto rack to cool before slicing. Makes 1 loaf.

ORANGE POPPY SEED BREAD

2 cups all-purpose flour
2 teaspoons baking powder
½ teaspoon salt
⅓ cup poppy seeds
½ cup (4 ounces/1 stick)
    butter, at room
    temperature
1 cup sugar

2 large eggs
1 cup milk
1 teaspoon vanilla
½ teaspoon orange extract
½ teaspoon almond extract
Grated zest of 1 medium
    orange

ADJUST OVEN RACK to top third position; preheat oven to 350°F. Coat 9 x 5 x 3-inch loaf pan with vegetable spray.

Thoroughly mix flour, baking powder, salt, and poppy seeds in medium bowl.

Cream butter and sugar in large bowl of electric mixer for 3 minutes or until light and fluffy. Beat in eggs, one at a time, then milk, vanilla, orange extract, almond extract, and orange zest. On low speed, blend in dry ingredients just until combined; do not overmix.

Spoon batter into prepared pan, smoothing it on top. Bake for 1 hour to 1 hour and 15 minutes or until tester comes out clean. Turn out onto rack to cool completely. Makes 1 loaf.

L ots of pretty poppy seeds in this luxurious, cake-like bread. Though wonderful with a spot of tea, iced tea, or homemade lemonade, it is equally delightful served for dessert.

Because cranberries are only available seasonally, I always purchase several bags of them at Thanksgiving and Christmastime, then freeze them in plastic bags – they keep well for up to a year. This way, I can prepare any number of cranberry breads and muffins any time of the year.

CRANBERRY BREAD WITH ORANGE GLAZE

2 cups all-purpose flour
2 teaspoons baking powder
½ teaspoon baking soda
½ teaspoon salt
¼ cup (2 ounces / ½ stick) butter, at room temperature
¾ cup sugar
2 large eggs
1 cup buttermilk

Finely grated zest of 1 medium orange
2 teaspoons vanilla
1 cup whole cranberries, partially thawed if frozen
¼ cup fresh orange juice
2 tablespoons sugar
Grated zest of 1 medium orange

ADJUST OVEN RACK to top third position; preheat oven to 350°F. Coat 9 x 5 x 3-inch loaf pan with vegetable spray.

Thoroughly mix flour, baking powder, baking soda, and salt in medium bowl.

Cream butter and sugar in large bowl of electric mixer for 3 minutes or until light and fluffy. Beat in eggs, one at a time, then buttermilk, orange zest, and vanilla. On low speed, blend in dry ingredients just until combined; do not overmix. Fold in cranberries.

Spoon batter into prepared pan, smoothing it on top. Bake for 1 hour or until tester comes out clean.

Meanwhile, stir orange juice and sugar in bowl until sugar is dissolved. When bread is removed from oven, immediately turn out onto large piece of foil and pierce top in several places with toothpick. Restir orange glaze and slowly drizzle over bread. Sprinkle top with grated zest and cool completely before slicing. Makes 1 loaf.

APRICOT ORANGE BREAD

1½ cups dried apricots,
    diced
1 cup fresh orange juice
2 cups all-purpose flour
½ cup sugar
2 teaspoons baking powder
½ teaspoon baking soda

½ teaspoon salt
2 large eggs
¼ cup (2 ounces/½ stick)
    butter, melted
¼ cup milk
Grated zest of 1
    medium-large orange

ADJUST OVEN RACK to top third position; preheat oven to
350°F. Coat 9 x 5 x 3-inch loaf pan with vegetable spray.
    Place diced apricots in medium heatproof bowl. Bring
orange juice just to a boil and pour over apricots; set aside.
    Thoroughly mix flour, sugar, baking powder, baking
soda, and salt in large bowl. In medium bowl, whisk eggs,
butter, milk, and orange zest until blended; stir in apricot
mixture. Pour liquid mixture over dry ingredients and fold
in with rubber spatula just until combined; do not overmix.
    Spoon batter into prepared pan, smoothing it on top.
Bake for 50 minutes or until tester comes out clean. Carefully turn out onto rack to cool completely before slicing.
Makes 1 loaf.

O*ne of my personal favorites,
this beguilingly aromatic
loaf – laced with orange-
colored apricots – is
absolutely luscious to eat.*

During the course of writing this book, many people offered me their recipe for banana bread. It's obviously the most popular quick bread and so it should be: this moist loaf is not only tasty but is also perfect for utilizing those inevitable overripe bananas. ♦ My version is classic and perfumes the house with its aroma while baking. ♦ Chopped dates may be substituted for the pecans if you wish.

BANANA PECAN BREAD

2 cups all-purpose flour
2 teaspoons baking powder
1 teaspoon baking soda
½ teaspoon salt
½ cup (4 ounces/1 stick) butter, at room temperature
1 cup sugar

2 large eggs
1 cup mashed ripe bananas (about 2)
¼ cup sour cream
1 teaspoon vanilla
½ cup pecan halves, chopped

ADJUST OVEN RACK to top third position; preheat oven to 350°F. Coat 9 x 5 x 3-inch loaf pan with vegetable spray.

Thoroughly mix flour, baking powder, baking soda, and salt in medium bowl.

Cream butter and sugar in large bowl of electric mixer for 3 minutes or until light and fluffy. Beat in eggs, one at a time, then blend in bananas, sour cream, and vanilla. On low speed, blend in dry ingredients just until combined; do not overmix. Fold in nuts.

Spoon batter into prepared pan, smoothing it on top. Bake for 1 hour or until tester comes out clean. Turn out onto rack to cool completely before slicing. Makes 1 loaf.

APPLESAUCE BREAD

1 cup unsweetened
   applesauce
¼ cup (2 ounces / ½ stick)
   butter, melted
¼ cup liquid honey
2 large eggs
1 teaspoon vanilla
¾ cup raisins

2 cups all-purpose flour
½ cup packed brown sugar
2 teaspoons baking powder
½ teaspoon salt
½ teaspoon ground
   cinnamon
½ teaspoon grated nutmeg

ADJUST OVEN RACK to top third position; preheat oven to 350°F. Coat 9 x 5 x 3-inch loaf pan with vegetable spray.

Whisk applesauce, butter, honey, eggs, and vanilla in medium bowl until well blended; stir in raisins.

Thoroughly mix flour, sugar, baking powder, salt, cinnamon, and nutmeg in large bowl. Pour liquid mixture over dry ingredients and fold in with rubber spatula just until combined; do not overmix.

Spoon batter into prepared pan, smoothing it on top. Bake for 50 minutes or until tester comes out clean. Carefully turn out onto rack to cool before slicing. Makes 1 loaf.

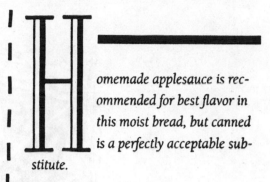

omemade applesauce is recommended for best flavor in this moist bread, but canned is a perfectly acceptable substitute.

loaf pans

SAVORY

QUICK BREADS

♦ ♦ ♦

Bright yellow cornmeal bread, flecked with jalapeños, coriander, and green onion looks simply gorgeous. ♦ The bread is scrumptious served warm or at room temperature spread with butter.

SOUTHWESTERN CORNMEAL BREAD

1½ cups all-purpose flour
½ cup yellow cornmeal
¼ cup sugar
2 teaspoons baking powder
1 teaspoon baking soda
1 teaspoon salt
2 large eggs
1 cup buttermilk
¼ cup (2 ounces/½ stick) butter, melted

¾ cup grated Cheddar cheese
¾ cup frozen corn, thawed
¼ cup pickled sliced jalapeños, diced
¼ cup finely chopped fresh coriander
1 large green onion (green part only), finely chopped

ADJUST OVEN RACK to top third position; preheat oven to 350°F. Coat 9 x 5 x 3-inch loaf pan with vegetable spray.

Thoroughly mix flour, cornmeal, sugar, baking powder, baking soda, and salt in large bowl. In medium bowl, whisk eggs, buttermilk, and butter until blended. Pour liquid mixture over dry ingredients and fold in with rubber spatula just until combined. Fold in cheese, corn, jalapeños, coriander, and green onion.

Spoon batter into prepared pan, smoothing it on top. Bake for 50 minutes or until tester comes out clean. Turn out onto rack, then slice and serve warm. Makes 1 loaf.

BACON AND ONION BREAD

5 to 6 strips bacon
1 small onion, chopped
2 cups all-purpose flour
1 tablespoon baking
   powder
1 tablespoon sugar
¼ teaspoon salt

⅛ teaspoon freshly ground
   black pepper
⅛ teaspoon cayenne
2 large eggs
1 cup sour cream
¼ cup (2 ounces / ½ stick)
   butter, melted

ADJUST OVEN RACK to top third position; preheat oven to 350°F. Coat 9 x 5 x 3-inch loaf pan with vegetable spray.

Cook bacon in small nonstick skillet just until crisp. Using slotted spoon, transfer to paper towel-lined plate to drain; then coarsely dice. Remove and discard all but 2 tablespoons fat. Add onion and cook for 2 minutes or until tender.

Thoroughly mix flour, baking powder, sugar, salt, pepper, and cayenne in large bowl. Whisk eggs, sour cream, and butter in medium bowl until blended; stir in bacon and onion. Pour liquid mixture over dry ingredients and fold in with rubber spatula just until combined; do not overmix.

Spoon batter into prepared loaf pan, smoothing it on top. Bake for 50 minutes or until tester comes out clean. Turn out onto rack to cool before slicing. Makes 1 loaf.

easoned with bacon and onion, this especially delicious, savory bread is wonderful with soups or omelets or simply as a snack. ♦ Use premium-quality bacon, the kind sold at butcher shops and farmer's markets, for best flavor.

Delicious on its own, with a meal, or with cheese as an afternoon snack. ◆ Don't chop the olives too fine, you want good-sized pieces for best flavor.

GREEN OLIVE BREAD

2 cups all-purpose flour
1 tablespoon sugar
2 teaspoons baking powder
¼ teaspoon salt
2 large eggs
½ cup (4 ounces/1 stick) butter, melted

½ cup milk
1½ cups (13.5-ounce jar) coarsely chopped pimiento-stuffed green olives, well drained and patted dry

ADJUST OVEN RACK to top third position; preheat oven to 350°F. Coat 9 x 5 x 3-inch loaf pan with vegetable spray.

Thoroughly mix flour, sugar, baking powder, and salt in large bowl. In medium bowl, whisk eggs, butter, and milk until blended; stir in olives. Pour liquid mixture over dry ingredients and fold in with rubber spatula just until combined; do not overmix.

Spoon batter into prepared pan, smoothing it on top. Bake for 50 minutes or until tester comes out clean. Carefully turn out onto rack to cool completely. Makes 1 loaf.

SUN-DRIED TOMATO AND OLIVE BREAD

¾ cup drained sun-dried
  tomatoes
½ cup black olives
  (Kalamata), pitted and
  coarsely chopped
2 tablespoons oil from
  sun-dried tomatoes
2 large garlic cloves, finely
  chopped
2 cups all-purpose flour
1 tablespoon sugar

2 teaspoons baking powder
1 teaspoon baking soda
¼ teaspoon salt
¼ teaspoon dried basil
2 large eggs
1 cup milk
¼ cup (2 ounces/½ stick)
  butter, melted
1 cup coarsely crumbled
  feta cheese

ADJUST OVEN RACK to top third position; preheat oven to 400°F. Coat 9 × 5 × 3-inch loaf pan with vegetable spray.

Coarsely chop sun-dried tomatoes and place in small bowl with chopped olives.

Heat sun-dried-tomato oil in small nonstick skillet over medium heat. Add garlic and cook 1 minute or until tender. Using rubber spatula, scrape oil and garlic into bowl with sun-dried tomatoes and olives.

Thoroughly mix flour, sugar, baking powder, baking soda, salt, and basil in large bowl. Whisk eggs, milk, and butter in medium bowl. Pour liquid mixture over dry ingredients; add sun-dried tomato mixture and cheese. Fold in with rubber spatula just until combined; do not overmix.

Spoon batter into prepared pan, smoothing it on top. Bake for 50 minutes or until tester comes out clean. Carefully turn out onto rack and allow to cool completely before slicing. Makes 1 loaf.

*O*lives, sun-dried tomatoes, and feta cheese combine to make a bread that's not for the faint of heart when it comes to assertive flavors. Fanciers of such (like me!) have been known to devour a slice or two for lunch or a snack.

BLACK
OLIVES

A*n easy, quick variation of yeast-risen rye bread.*

CARAWAY RYE BREAD

1 cup rye flour
1 cup all-purpose flour
2 tablespoons brown sugar
2 teaspoons baking powder
½ teaspoon baking soda
½ teaspoon salt

1 tablespoon caraway seeds
2 large eggs
1 cup sour cream
¼ cup (2 ounces/½ stick)
   butter, melted

ADJUST OVEN RACK to top third position; preheat oven to 350°F. Coat 9 x 5 x 3-inch loaf with vegetable spray.

Thoroughly mix rye flour, all-purpose flour, brown sugar, baking powder, baking soda, salt, and caraway seeds in large bowl. Whisk eggs, sour cream, and butter in medium bowl until blended. Pour liquid mixture over dry ingredients and fold in with rubber spatula just until combined; do not overmix.

Spoon batter into prepared pan, smoothing it on top. Bake for 50 minutes or until tester comes out clean. Turn out onto rack to cool before slicing. Makes 1 loaf.

BOSTON BROWN BREAD

1 cup whole wheat flour	2 large eggs
1 cup all-purpose flour	1¼ cups buttermilk
1 cup yellow cornmeal	¼ cup (2 ounces / ½ stick)
2 teaspoons baking powder	butter, melted
¾ teaspoon salt	⅓ cup molasses
½ teaspoon baking soda	½ cup raisins

ADJUST OVEN RACK to top third position; preheat oven to 350°F. Coat 9 x 5 x 3-inch loaf pan with vegetable spray.

Thoroughly mix flours, cornmeal, baking powder, salt, and baking soda in large bowl. Whisk eggs, buttermilk, butter, and molasses in medium bowl. Pour liquid mixture over dry ingredients and add raisins; fold in with rubber spatula just until combined; do not overmix.

Spoon batter into prepared loaf pan, smoothing it on top. Bake for 1 hour or until tester comes out clean. Cool in pan on rack for 10 minutes, then turn out onto rack and serve warm or at room temperature. Makes 1 loaf.

Classic Boston bread is a hearty, textural, dark-colored loaf. Traditionally steamed rather than baked and served alongside Boston baked beans, it is also a delicious breakfast accompaniment served warm from the oven or toasted – with butter.

A quick-to-assemble garlic bread to serve with your favorite barbecue or Italian dinner.

GARLIC BREAD

2 cups all-purpose flour
1 tablespoon sugar
2 teaspoons baking powder
2 teaspoons dried basil
½ teaspoon baking soda
½ teaspoon salt

2 large eggs
¾ cup milk
¼ cup (2 ounces/½ stick) butter, melted
1 large garlic clove, minced

ADJUST OVEN RACK to top third position; preheat oven to 350°F. Coat 9 x 5 x 3-inch loaf pan with vegetable spray.

Thoroughly combine flour, sugar, baking powder, basil, baking soda, and salt in large bowl. Whisk eggs, milk, butter, and garlic in medium bowl until blended. Pour liquid mixture over dry ingredients and fold in with rubber spatula just until combined.

Spoon batter into prepared pan, smoothing it on top. Bake for 50 minutes or until tester comes out clean. Turn out onto rack, slice, and serve warm. Makes 1 small loaf.

POPOVERS, SCONES & BISCUITS

◆ ◆ ◆

Crystallized ginger is available in some bulk food and Asian food stores. ◆ Serve Ginger Scones with your best and rarest tea.

GINGER SCONES

2 cups all-purpose flour
1 tablespoon baking
   powder
1 tablespoon sugar
½ teaspoon salt
¼ cup (2 ounces / ½ stick)
   chilled butter, diced

1 large egg
1 cup heavy cream plus
   extra for glazing
½ cup chopped crystallized
   ginger

ADJUST OVEN RACK to top third position; preheat oven to 400°F. Lightly coat baking sheet with vegetable spray.

Thoroughly mix flour, baking powder, sugar, and salt in large bowl. Add butter and crumble mixture with your fingers until it resembles very coarse meal. Whisk egg and cream in medium bowl and stir in ginger. Pour liquid mixture over dry ingredients and fold in with rubber spatula just until combined; do not overmix.

Turn out onto floured surface and place large piece of plastic wrap over dough. Roll dough to ¾-inch thickness and remove plastic wrap. Cut out rounds with 2-inch floured cutter and transfer to prepared baking sheet. Brush tops with a little cream. Bake for 15 minutes or until tops are pale golden and tester comes out clean. Serve warm. Makes about 12 scones.

AFTERNOON TEA SCONES

2 cups all-purpose flour
¼ cup sugar
1 tablespoon baking
    powder
1 teaspoon salt
¼ cup (2 ounces/½ stick)
    chilled butter, diced

1 large egg
1 cup heavy cream plus
    extra for glazing
½ cup currants

ADJUST OVEN RACK to top third position; preheat oven to 400°F. Lightly coat baking sheet with vegetable spray.

Thoroughly mix flour, sugar, baking powder, and salt in large bowl. Add butter and crumble mixture with your fingers until it resembles very coarse meal. Whisk egg and cream in medium bowl and stir in currants. Pour liquid mixture over dry ingredients and fold in with rubber spatula just until combined; do not overmix.

Turn out onto floured surface and place large piece of plastic wrap over dough. Roll dough to ¼-inch thickness and remove plastic wrap. Cut out rounds with 2-inch floured cutter and transfer to prepared baking sheet. Brush tops with a little cream. Bake for 15 minutes or until pale golden and tester comes out clean. Serve warm. Makes about 12 scones.

These sophisticated, rich scones are perfect for an elegant tea party. (They're just fabulous with ice-cold lemonade, too.) The perfect accompaniment: a dollop of Devonshire, thick double cream, or some sweet butter. ◆ For those who prefer a less sweet scone, reduce sugar by half.

Heavy cast-iron popover pans work best, though sometimes I like to make miniature Yorkshire puddings by baking them in mini-muffin pans. ♦ Serve the puddings with roast beef and gravy.

MOM'S YORKSHIRE PUDDING

2 large eggs
1 cup milk
1 cup all-purpose flour

½ teaspoon salt
Beef drippings

ADD EGGS, milk, flour, and salt to blender. Cover and process on low speed. Stop blender, scrape down sides of container, and blend again on high speed for a few seconds or until smooth. (For best results, allow to stand for 30 minutes to 1 hour.)

When roast is removed from oven, adjust oven rack to top third position and turn heat to 475°F.

Spoon about 1 teaspoon beef drippings into each of 8 popover cups. Place pan in oven a few minutes to get very hot. Watch carefully. Remove pan from oven and immediately pour batter into prepared cups, filling each about two-thirds full. Bake for 10 minutes, then reduce heat to 400°F, and bake for 20 minutes more or until puffed, brown, and crisp. (Don't open oven until popovers are fully baked or they won't rise.) Serve at once. Makes 8 popovers.

POPOVERS

3 large eggs
1 cup milk
1 cup all-purpose flour

2 tablespoons melted butter
½ teaspoon salt

ADD EGGS, milk, flour, butter, and salt to blender. Cover and process on low speed. Stop blender, scrape down sides of container, and blend again on high speed for a few seconds or until smooth. (For best results, allow to stand for 30 minutes to 1 hour.)

Adjust oven rack to top third position; preheat oven to 475°F. Place cast-iron popover pan in oven to heat for a few minutes. Remove hot pan from oven; generously coat with vegetable spray.

Immediately pour batter into prepared cups, filling each about two-thirds full. Bake for 10 minutes, then reduce heat to 400°F and bake 15 minutes more or until puffed, brown, and crisp. (Don't open oven until popovers are fully baked or they won't rise.) Serve at once. Makes about 8 popovers.

F*resh, hot popovers are yummy for breakfast and should be served as soon as they come out of the oven. Break one open, slather with soft butter, dollop your favorite jam onto each half and eat at once!*

different twist on the popover theme. ◆ *Serve with roast chicken and gravy.*

CORNMEAL POPOVERS

3 large eggs   ½ cup yellow cornmeal
1 cup milk   3 tablespoons melted butter
½ cup all-purpose flour   ½ teaspoon salt

ADD EGGS, milk, flour, cornmeal, butter, and salt to blender. Cover and process on low speed. Stop blender, scrape down sides of container, and blend again on high speed for a few seconds or until smooth. (For best results, allow to stand for 30 minutes to 1 hour.)

Adjust oven rack to top third position; preheat oven to 475°F. Place cast-iron popover pan in oven to heat. Remove pan from oven; generously coat with vegetable spray.

Reblend batter; immediately pour batter into prepared cups, filling each about two-thirds full. Bake for 10 minutes, then reduce heat to 400°F and bake 15 minutes more or until puffed, brown, and crisp. (Don't open oven until popovers are fully baked or they won't rise.) Serve at once. Makes 8 popovers.

PARMESAN BASIL POPOVERS

2 large eggs
1 cup milk
1 cup all-purpose flour
2 tablespoons melted butter

⅓ cup freshly grated
 Parmesan cheese
½ teaspoon dried basil

ADD EGGS, milk, flour, butter, Parmesan cheese, and basil to blender. Cover and process on low speed. Stop blender, scrape down sides of container, and blend again on high speed for a few seconds or until smooth. (For best results, allow to stand for 30 minutes to 1 hour.)

Adjust oven rack to top third position; preheat oven to 475°F. Place cast-iron popover pan in oven to heat for a few minutes. Remove hot pan from oven; generously coat with vegetable spray.

Reblend batter; immediately pour batter into prepared cups, filling each about two-thirds full. Bake for 10 minutes, then reduce heat to 400°F and bake 15 minutes more or until puffed, brown, and crisp. (Don't open oven until popovers are fully baked or they won't rise.) Serve at once. Makes about 8 popovers.

P opovers are fun to experiment with, adding different ingredients on a whim. ♦ I created these to serve with an Italian lunch or supper.

cheese grater

Popovers filled with buttery
blue cheese are an uncommon
accompaniment to lunch or
dinner or an assertively-
flavored salad such as a Caesar. ♦ For
a more delicate taste, you may replace
the Gorgonzola with goat cheese instead.

GORGONZOLA POPOVERS

2 large eggs   ½ teaspoon salt
1 cup milk   About 6 ounces
1 cup all-purpose flour   Gorgonzola cheese,
2 tablespoons melted butter   divided into 8 pieces

ADD EGGS, milk, flour, butter, and salt to blender. Cover
and process on low speed,. Stop blender, scrape down sides
of container, and blend again on high speed for a few
seconds or until smooth. (For best results, allow to stand
for 30 minutes to 1 hour.)

Adjust oven rack to top third position; preheat oven to
475°F. Place cast-iron popover pan in oven to heat for a few
minutes. Remove hot pan from oven; generously coat with
vegetable spray.

Immediately pour batter into prepared cups, filling each
about two-thirds full. Place a piece of cheese in center of
each one. Bake for 10 minutes, then reduce heat to 400°F
and bake 15 minutes more or until puffed, brown, and
crisp. (Don't open oven until popovers are fully baked or
they won't rise.) Serve at once. Makes about 8 popovers.

BUTTERMILK BISCUITS

2 cups all-purpose flour
1 tablespoon baking
  powder
2 teaspoons sugar
1 teaspoon baking soda

½ teaspoon salt
½ cup chilled butter, diced
¾ cup buttermilk plus extra
  for glazing

PREHEAT OVEN to 400°F.

Thoroughly mix flour, baking powder, sugar, baking soda, and salt in large bowl. Add butter and crumble mixture with your fingers until it resembles very coarse meal. Pour buttermilk over dry mixture and fold in with rubber spatula just until combined. Turn out onto lightly floured surface and place a large piece of plastic wrap over dough. Roll dough to 1¼-inch thickness and remove plastic wrap. Cut with 2-inch floured cutter and place on ungreased baking sheet.

Brush tops with a little buttermilk. Bake for 15 minutes or until tops are golden and tester comes out clean. Serve at once. Makes about 8 biscuits.

For these tender, high biscuits, the secret is to roll the dough to 1¼-inch thickness – not the typical ¾-inch thickness – and to place the dough circles touching each other on the baking sheet, which produces tender biscuits. If you prefer crisp-edged biscuits, space them 1 inch apart on the baking sheet.

INDEX

◆ ◆ ◆